PRAISE FOR *TRANSFORM TEACHING AND LEARNING THROUGH TALK: THE ORACY IMPERATIVE*

"Here's a book overflowing with ideas of how to make oracy come alive in the classroom. It will be welcomed by all heads of department who want to enable their children to lead fulfilled and successful lives—and do well in their exams! Although it doesn't set out explicitly to do so, it is also a 'vade mecum' for teachers wishing to make tutor periods fun and valuable. The many cogent examples of 'how-to-do-it' are drawn from classroom practice and will be gobbled up by teachers looking for practical ideas.

The two authors who hail from the pioneering School 21 also justify the importance of oracy, which strangely (given their reliance on oracy) appeals only fitfully to politicians making national policy. Yet listening and speaking are a precondition of a free and democratic society and a vital part of everybody's claim to be educated. After all until a person with a case which is just can argue it in a way which might enable it to prevail, there will continue to exist a mental form of slavery that is as real as any economic form. Teachers are pledged to destroy such slavery.

This book will help them immeasurably in their vital task and should be on the shelf of every school's staff library."—**Professor Tim Brighouse, former chief commissioner for schools**

"High-quality talk in classrooms is easier to describe than to put into action. This book sets out in meticulous detail the what, the why and the how of securing great quality talk in classrooms. It leaves no stone unturned, draws extensively on the research and offers examples of how high-quality oracy and its cousin, listening, work in classrooms. This is a rich, carefully structured resource, and will be a boon to individual teachers and whole school communities who know the importance of strengthening this aspect of their practice."—**Mary Myatt, education advisor**

Transform Teaching and Learning through Talk

The Oracy Imperative

AMY GAUNT
ALICE STOTT

ROWMAN & LITTLEFIELD
Lanham • Boulder • New York • London

Published by Rowman & Littlefield
An imprint of The Rowman & Littlefield Publishing Group, Inc.
4501 Forbes Boulevard, Suite 200, Lanham, Maryland 20706
www.rowman.com

Unit A, Whitacre Mews, 26-34 Stannary Street, London SE11 4AB

British Library Cataloguing in Publication Information Available

Library of Congress Cataloging-in-Publication Data

Names: Gaunt, Amy, 1987– author. | Stott, Alice, 1991– author.
Title: Transform teaching and learning through talk : the oracy imperative /
  Amy Gaunt, Alice Stott.
Description: Lanham, Maryland : Rowman & Littlefield, [2019] | Includes
  bibliographical references and index.
Identifiers: LCCN 2018036270 (print) | LCCN 2018048079 (ebook) | ISBN
  9781475840698 (electronic) | ISBN 9781475840674 (cloth : alk. paper) |
  ISBN 9781475840681 (pbk. : alk. paper)
Subjects: LCSH: Forums (Discussion and debate) | Discussion—Study and
  teaching. | Inquiry-based learning. | Interaction analysis in education.
Classification: LCC LC6519 (ebook) | LCC LC6519 .G38 2019 (print) | DDC
  371.3/7—dc23
LC record available at https://lccn.loc.gov/2018036270

♾™ The paper used in this publication meets the minimum requirements of
American National Standard for Information Sciences—Permanence of Paper
for Printed Library Materials, ANSI/NISO Z39.48-1992.

Printed in the United States of America

To the ever-inspiring students
and teachers at School 21

Contents

Foreword

The ability to speak eloquently, articulate ideas and thoughts, influence through talking, collaborate with peers, and have the confidence to express your views are vital skills that support success in learning and life in general. In 2012, the founders of School 21 observed the lack of attention given to the development of students' spoken communication in the majority of state schools. Establishing a new comprehensive school for children aged four to eighteen, they set out on a mission to give oracy the same status as literacy and numeracy in the education they provide for the children and young people of the school's local community of East London, England.

By embedding oracy in all aspects of the school's culture and weaving it throughout the curriculum, they demonstrated that the deliberate and explicit teaching of speaking and listening supports progress and achievement. Throughout the school, classrooms buzz with the sound of purposeful talk, from five-year-olds learning how to take turns and effectively participate in discussions to seventeen-year-olds sitting in circles, dissecting the arguments for and against referendums as a decision-making tool. The visitors to the school are consistently amazed by the quality of the dialogue, ambitious vocabulary, and sense of agency exhibited by the students. It was in these classrooms that I first met Amy and Alice.

As teachers and leaders of oracy across School 21, it was their responsibility to work with colleagues from different subjects and phases to understand the active ingredients of effective oracy teaching and ensure that all teachers in the school had the awareness, expertise, and knowledge to use them.

As more schools started to recognize the benefits of this focus on spoken communication, School 21 set up a sister charity, Voice 21, to share these approaches beyond the school's gates and Amy and Alice joined as our codirectors of Teaching and Learning. So alongside writing this book, they have been busy traveling the length and breadth of the UK, supporting thousands of teachers and hundreds of schools to embrace oracy in their pedagogy and curriculum.

Working with a diversity of schools, across different geographies and demographics, has helped Alice and Amy to further hone in on the key aspects all teachers need to consider when creating the conditions for high-quality talk in their classrooms. Rooted in the realities of teaching, it is the questions, experiences, concerns, and inspiration of these educators that have shaped this book.

Through these approaches, students will develop the skills to listen effectively, discuss and respond with meaning, and debate and disagree agreeably. As they become able to explain ideas and emotions to other people, not only in a school setting but in their lives outside the classroom, too, they will gain the confidence, self-belief, and courage to speak in public and share their thoughts, intellect, and creativity with the world.

Whether you are just setting out on your career in teaching or have many years of experience, this book will challenge you to think deeply about what you can do to integrate oracy into your practice. Rich with ideas, advice, and strategies, *Transform Teaching and Learning through Talk: The Oracy Imperative* will quickly become your go-to guide to get talking in class!

Beccy Earnshaw
Director, Voice 21

Acknowledgments

There are many people we would like to thank for helping this book become a reality. This book wouldn't exist if it wasn't for the vision and leadership of the founders of School 21: Ed Fidoe, Oli de Botton, and Peter Hyman. In creating a school with speaking at its heart, they enabled and empowered the school's teachers to forge a talk-rich approach to teaching that values and develops every child's voice.

We owe particular thanks to the school's founding teachers who weaved oracy into the fabric of the school, creating the blueprint for an oracy education that many other schools now seek to emulate and adapt. It's thanks to these strong foundations that we have been able to build our understanding of oracy and approach to teaching this important skill. We'd like to thank the pioneering and innovative teachers at both School 21 and at schools across the UK who have been generous in sharing their own ideas as well as trying out and evaluating ours.

We have also learned a huge amount from the work of the academics and authors who have shaped this field. Most notably, Neil Mercer, Douglas Barnes, Robin Alexander, Lyn Dawes, Frank Hardman, and Rupert Weigerif, who have been formative in shaping our understanding of the role of talk in the classroom and to whom we owe a great deal.

Finally, we'd also like to say a massive thank you to the whole Voice 21 team who are a constant source of encouragement and inspiration. In particular, Beccy Earnshaw, for challenging us to think harder and more deeply and for always believing in us, and Lizzie Lynch, for her skilful design work and endless patience!

Introduction

It's Monday morning. Over the weekend London has faced a second terrorist attack in as many months. Understandably, the students of Seacole Class are shaken. Many of them arrive early for school, impatient to talk about—to try and make sense of—what has happened. The morning's lessons are abandoned, and instead a class meeting is convened. The students sit in a circle, patiently offering out their thumbs to indicate they have something to say. The first student begins, "I just don't know why anyone would do this. I feel angry."

Over the next forty-five minutes unfolds a truly remarkable discussion. The students, from different backgrounds, representing a number of different religions, proceed to explain how this attack misrepresented Islam and defied their understanding of humanity. As the discussion develops, students identify and explore the values they each hold, engaging with each other's perspectives and using these ideas to revise their own point of view. Finally, the students skillfully reach a consensus, concluding that many of the divisions in society could be overcome if people only took the time to talk and, perhaps more importantly, to listen to each other.

Listening to a class of eight- and nine-year-olds discuss such a contentious and delicate issue, with a sensitivity and maturity beyond their years, was a transformational moment. If everybody was able to discuss difficult issues in such a thoughtful and measured way, then the world would be a richer, more tolerant, less divided place.

As a teacher, it is these moments, when your students join the dots, when everything comes together and they just "get it," that make teaching worthwhile. However, powerful learning episodes like these do not happen by chance. The discussion described above is an example of what students can achieve when oracy skills are deliberately and explicitly taught and when students have opportunities to use these skills to explore issues that are meaningful to them.

Talk has always been integral to our classroom practice, for different reasons. As a teacher working with students in their first years of school, Amy has always understood talk as a tool for learning, whether asking students to speak with their "talk partner," work collaboratively with their peers, or explain their ideas clearly and succinctly.

Similarly, as an English teacher working with older students, language—whether spoken, written, or read—was always a focus in Alice's classroom. Having taught debate at inner-city London schools, and having loved it as a teenager, she often brought speaking and techniques from debating into her lessons.

However, it is only since joining School 21 that we have come to understand the true significance of talk in the classroom. When students are provided with opportunities to engage in meaningful talk, and teachers have a framework to understand and teach it, the impact on learning is profound. If this is coupled with plenty of chances for pupils to use their voice in different contexts, rehearsing and refining their talk for different audiences, the effect on learning can be transformative.

As leaders of oracy across School 21 (a school serving students from age four to eighteen), working with teachers of different subjects and age groups has enabled us to see the impact of oracy on teaching and learning not just in our own classrooms, but across the wider curriculum. Through our work with Voice 21, a charity committed to raising the status of oracy in education, we have supported hundreds of teachers and schools to develop their teaching of oracy, enabling us to see firsthand the impact this work can have in any school.

We hope that this book serves as a guide to help you embed oracy in your classroom and in doing so enable your students to find their voices. As you read, you will find plenty of practical ideas to do just this in the "Oracy in

Action" boxes. To bring these to life, we have also included a number of case studies that give real and relatable examples from our own classrooms.

The book is organized sequentially, outlining first how to build a culture of classroom talk before moving on to planning and teaching the more presentational aspects of talk. We would therefore encourage you, on first consideration, to read the chapters in order. For some readers, the ideas and approaches outlined may not be entirely new; however, reading the book sequentially will give you a deeper understanding of how oracy can be planned for deliberately, taught explicitly, and engaged in consciously.

Throughout this book we use the terms *oracy, talk,* and *speaking* interchangeably, and to encompass their sister skill of listening, which is the necessary flip side to speaking. However, a more detailed examination of the skills specific to listening, and how these can be taught, can be found in chapter 8, "Teach Listening, Too."

We hope that this book sparks a long-standing interest in oracy and that you have fun trying out the approaches and practical activities shared in your own classroom. We have used the activities included with a range of students of different ages, but we very much encourage you to adapt them for your students, as well as to create your own.

Let's get talking in class!

1

Take Speaking Seriously

Oracy enables students to find their voice both metaphorically and literally.

—*Peter Hyman, Executive Head Teacher, School 21*

Our ability to use speech to express our thoughts and communicate with others is one of the qualities that makes us uniquely human. From infancy, babies learn the power of their voice to communicate their basic wants and needs. As we grow older, our use of voice becomes more sophisticated. It is through spoken language that we make meaning, build relationships, and interact with the world around us. Talk is such an essential part of our everyday existence that it is easy to engage in it unthinkingly. However, to neglect spoken language in the classroom does a disservice to the young people we teach.

Oracy is an ugly word, but the choice to use it in this text (and in the classroom) is deliberate. It was first coined by academic Andrew Wilkinson in the 1960s, in direct response to the growing importance placed on literacy and numeracy. It captures the essential *need* for talk (just as one needs to be literate and numerate) and couples it with the idea that it is a skill that can be acquired through teaching.

While no one would ever question the need to teach a child to read, all too often it is assumed that speaking is a skill that doesn't require teaching—instead, children should just "pick it up." But not all children will.

Evidence shows that of the children who persistently experienced poverty, 75 percent arrive at school below average in language development.[1] If students do not acquire this language at home, school is, as Neil Mercer explains, their second chance: "If they are not getting it in school, they are not getting it."[2] Oracy, therefore, is not just an educational choice but a moral imperative.

The implications of an oracy education are far-reaching. There is a compelling case for the role of oracy in improving educational outcomes. Through verbally elaborating on their ideas, building on the contributions of others, and questioning the basis of each other's thinking, students actively engage in and monitor their own learning, deepening their understanding of concepts and ideas.

The cognitive benefits of oracy are reflected in the robust evidence that quality classroom talk has a measurable impact on academic attainment.[3] These benefits include greater retention of subject-specific knowledge, vocabulary acquisition, and reasoning skills[4] and are not merely confined to subjects traditionally associated with discussion and dialogue, such as the arts and humanities. The benefits of talk-rich teaching and learning can be found across the curriculum, in mathematics and science.[5]

Moreover, the skills developed through oracy are transferred into other subjects and contexts.[6] For instance, teaching children to talk together in order to solve problems improves their reasoning skills, not only when working as a group, but also when working independently.[7]

The benefits of oracy teaching also extend beyond the classroom, supporting the development of students' confidence and self-esteem.[8] Creating a space in which students can express their ideas, and know that these will be listened to and valued, sends a powerful message to the young people you teach.

As one child put it, "What makes me enjoy talking the most is that everybody's listening to you, and you're part of the world, and you feel respected and important" (seven-year-old School 21 student). Placing value on students' ideas and opinions not only contributes toward their sense of self-worth, but also builds a greater sense of community and belonging in school.[9]

A focus on your students' "voice," in the broadest sense of the word, also contributes toward shaping active, engaged, thoughtful, and reflective citizenry. As Professor Robin Alexander states, "Talk is a fundamental prerequisite for democratic engagement."[10] It is through talk that much of civic life and democratic dialogue are conducted. In an increasingly polarized world, young people must leave school able to deliberate, reason, and negotiate through listening to and talking with others.

The oracy skills acquired by students at school are also highly valuable upon leaving school and entering the world of work. Good grades and qualifications may get a candidate to an interview, but it will be their performance in the interview that lands them the job. To suggest to young people that hard work and good grades alone are enough to land jobs in the top professions does a disservice to young people who will need to be able to navigate the unwritten social codes of interviews and networking with confidence.

Consistently, surveys show that verbal communication skills and teamwork are sought after by employers, and yet are the most lacking in school leavers.[11] In 2015 almost half of British employers reported concerns with the communication skills of young people entering the workplace.[12] Without a focus on oracy, schools risk not adequately equipping young people with the communication, presentation, and interpersonal skills needed to thrive in the twenty-first-century workplace.

As the qualities developed through oracy are so desirable—in particular the ability to speak articulately, with confidence and fluency—it is perhaps no coincidence that teachers at fee-based schools place far greater emphasis on developing their students' verbal communication skills than their state-funded counterparts.[13]

This risks widening the gap between the "haves" and "have nots": children from privileged backgrounds are also taught to talk at school, while those from disadvantaged backgrounds who arrive at school with less language have less opportunity to acquire it. This is borne out in the data: those who start school behind in language are the least likely to catch up.[14]

Speaking skills must be taught rather than simply "caught" by a fortunate few. Although as teachers we cannot control the amount of language students arrive at school with, or what happens beyond the school gates to change this, we *do* have control over what happens in our classrooms. The power to create language-rich classrooms filled with talk is in our hands.

Consider how you use your voice: to negotiate and make decisions with colleagues, to instruct your students, to play with your children, or to entertain your friends. When your students leave school, they will need to be agile communicators who are able to navigate the varied and implicit expectations for talk in different contexts.

Many people assume that teaching talk centers around high-stakes, formal, presentational situations where a speaker overcomes her fears to address an audience. This is of course an element of oracy. However, the range of situations in which one speaks across a day, let alone a lifetime, are far more varied than this.

Oracy is therefore a set of teachable skills that are essential for life, but it is also a pedagogy. When used skillfully, talk allows students to take ownership of their own learning, unlock and deepen their understanding, and think critically, giving students greater agency in the classroom.

Robin Alexander has written extensively on this dialogic ideal, exploring how teachers can employ dialogue in their classrooms and create the necessary conditions for educationally productive talk to thrive. Dialogic teaching "emphasises dialogue through which pupils learn to reason, discuss, argue, and explain in order to develop their higher order thinking as well as their articulacy."[15] Alexander emphasizes the importance of both teacher-student and student-student interactions. This book is primarily concerned with improving the quality of student-student interactions; however, this also has significant implications for your role as a teacher and will undoubtedly impact the way you interact with your students.

In this book, oracy is understood as both learning *to* talk and *through* talk. It is *through* talk that students use their collective thinking power to build and revise their understanding, negotiate complex ideas, and problem solve. This could be driven through interactions with peers or with teachers who, through their questioning, guide students to engage in higher-order thinking.

However, if students do not have the capabilities needed to engage in this paradigm, the benefits of classroom talk are limited. It is therefore essential that students are also taught *to* talk, ensuring that they have the necessary skills and understanding to engage in purposeful talk for learning. Figure 1.1 captures the interrelationship between learning *to* and *through* talk.

The best oracy teaching and learning takes place when students are both learning *through* and *to* talk. This is when students are negotiating and developing their subject knowledge and understanding *through* talk, which has been set up and scaffolded in such a way that they are also learning the skills needed *to* talk effectively.

Consider how this might look in practice. The first example that comes to mind is a discussion—often called upon by teachers across ages and subjects. Assuming the topic is subject specific and challenging, students engaged in

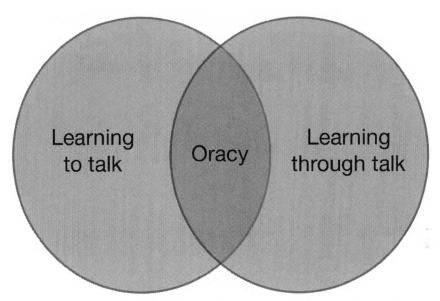

FIGURE 1.1
Oracy: Learning To and Through Talk

the discussion are learning *through* talk. However, the students would be getting more from their involvement if they were simultaneously learning *to* talk, in this case if their teacher had explicitly taught them the skills needed to engage in successful discussion, perhaps also providing them with scaffolds to support them to make meaningful contributions. A specific example of how this might look in practice is explored further in Box 1.1.

Bringing together these two layers of teaching, knowledge and skill, "what" and "how," pulls this learning experience into the middle sweet spot of the Venn diagram where learning *through* talk and *to* talk intersect.

An alternative example could be students presenting their understanding of a topic to an audience. An example of this is outlined in Box 1.2. By deciding on the salient points to share and explaining these accurately and succinctly, they are deepening their understanding of the subject at hand and are therefore learning *through* talk. If they have also been explicitly and carefully taught the conventions needed for this type of presentation, and have considered how best to engage their audience, this is also a moment when they are learning *to* talk.

You may already teach your students through talk, or at times to talk. However, effective oracy teaching and learning concerns how these two elements can be brought together to transform teaching and learning in your classroom.

BOX 1.1

DISCUSSION: LEARNING TO AND THROUGH TALK

Student A: I agree and disagree with this statement because, erm, sometimes children should be allowed to use the internet for their homework 'cause if you need to know something and you're not that sure then obviously you will go to the internet. I disagree because sometimes when a kid says that I'm going to use the internet, sometimes they lie and just watch some of their favorite movies.

Student B: I disagree with this statement because if children use the internet every day they could be doing stuff, like if they were downloading a game by using the internet and they never knew they were paying for the game, the consequences could be serious.

Student C: Well I agree and I also disagree, the same as what [Student A] said. Linking on to what you said, it's true that other people can, like, use the internet every day but some people don't have internet access so they won't be able to use it every day. What I think personally is that children should be able to use the internet because if they don't they will lose lots of knowledge and won't be able to find out things that they do not know.

Student D: I disagree and agree with the statement and would like to start by challenging [Student C]. You don't *always* have to use the internet to learn *everything*. You're a child—go to school, ask your teachers, your parents probably know some things too. I agree with this because can't we use the internet for free time to relax, watch your favorite YouTuber or play a game online?

In this extract from a transcript, nine-year-old students in my class discuss the statement "Children should not be allowed to use the internet." This is a topic they had been learning about as part of their personal and social education curriculum, and the discussion in question provides a forum for them to deepen their understanding of the risks involved in using the internet, and balance them against the benefits of responsible internet use; they are learning *through* talk.

However, these students are also learning *to* talk. In this example, they are embedding the skills needed for discussion that they have been explicitly taught. Notice how different students open their sentences "I agree and I disagree because . . ." "I think . . ." and "Linking on to what you said . . ." These are all scaffolds the students have been taught that enable them to contribute to a focused, extended discussion and offer alternative points of view.

Similarly, several students give reasons for their opinions in order to strengthen their case. It is also noticeable that the students are listening to each other and are clearly responding to what other speakers have said. This is most clearly seen when Student D challenges Student C's idea, but also when students reference another speaker's idea directly, as Student B does.

—*Amy Gaunt*

PRESENTATION: LEARNING TO AND THROUGH TALK

I worked with a teacher of science to devise a sequence of learning that would enable students to speak in role as geologists to demonstrate the effect of tectonic plate movement to a younger audience. This of course required the students to have a strong knowledge of how the earth's tectonic plates move, their different boundaries, and the impact this has on the earth's inhabitants.

Toward the end of the sequence of learning, once students were equipped with the key vocabulary and knowledge needed, they were then given the challenge of explaining this process to a group of younger students, using only Oreo cookies to demonstrate!

Students therefore had to think carefully about how they sequenced their ideas logically, the selection of appropriate vocabulary for their audience and how this was introduced, and how to present the content in an engaging manner (they were learning *to* talk). Sharing their knowledge in a different context required students to grapple with and consolidate their own understanding (they were learning *through* talk).

—*Alice Stott*

QUESTIONS TO CONSIDER
- Why does oracy matter for the students that you teach?
- How do you currently provide opportunities for your students to learn through and to talk?

NOTES
1. Communication Trust, *Talking about a Generation: Current Policy, Evidence and Practice for Speech, Language and Communication* (London: Communication Trust, 2017), http://www.thecommunicationtrust.org.uk/media/540327/tct_talkingaboutageneration_report_online.pdf.

2. N. Mercer, "How Much of Your Lesson Should Be Teacher Talk?" April 25, 2018, *Tes Podagogy,* https://tesnews.podbean.com/e/how-much-of-your-lesson -should-be-teacher-talk-professor-neil-mercer-talks-to-tes-podagogy.

3. R. Alexander, "Improving Oracy and Classroom Talk in English Schools: Achievements and Challenges" (presented at Department for Education seminar on oracy, February 20, 2012), http://www.robinalexander.org.uk/wp-content/ uploads/2012/06/DfE-oracy-120220-Alexander-FINAL.pdf.

4. W. Millard and L. Menzies, *The State of Speaking in Our Schools* (London: Voice 21/LKMCo, 2016), 22, https://www.esu.org/__data/assets/pdf_ file/0026/13796/Oracy-State-of-speaking-report-v2.pdf.

5. T. Jay, B. Willis, P. Thomas, R. Taylor, N. Moore, C. Burnett, G. Merchant, and A. Stevens. *Dialogic Teaching: Evaluation Report and Executive Summary* (London: Education Endowment Foundation, 2017), https://educationendowmentfoundation .org.uk/public/files/Projects/Evaluation_Reports/Dialogic_Teaching_Evaluation_ Report.pdf.

6. Millard and Menzies, *State of Speaking,* 22.

7. N. Mercer, R. Wegerif, and L. Dawes, "Children's Talk and the Development of Reasoning in the Classroom," *British Educational Research Journal* 25 (1999), 95–111.

8. Millard and Menzies, *State of Speaking,* 30.

9. J. Smith, A. Grant, N. Horrocks, K. Seymour, A. Boyle, L. Bardwell, and M. Turner. *Voice 21: Pilot Report and Executive Summary* (London: Education Endowment Foundation, 2018), 33, https://educationendowmentfoundation.org.uk/ public/files/Projects/Evaluation_Reports/Voice_21.pdf.

10. As quoted in Millard and Menzies, *State of Speaking,* 34.

11. Millard and Menzies, *State of Speaking.*

12. CBI/Pearson, *Inspiring Growth: CBI/Pearson Education and Skills Survey 2015* (London: CBI, 2015), 37, http://www.cbi.org.uk/cbi-prod/assets/File/Education-and -skills-survey-2015.pdf.

13. Millard and Menzies, *State of Speaking,* 26.

14. Communication Trust, *Talking about a Generation.*

15. Jay et al., *Dialogic Teaching,* 4.

Know What Makes Good Talk

Great speakers are made, not born. With the right teaching and support, all students can become confident, fluent speakers able to express themselves eloquently in a range of different contexts. To teach students to become great speakers, it is important to first understand the skills that make for good oracy. It is also important to recognize that the hallmarks of good oracy change according to the context in which someone is speaking. For example, the skills necessary to give an expert talk to a large audience are very different than those required to negotiate a complex issue in a group.

The Oracy Framework[1] (see Figure 2.1), devised by Cambridge University and teachers at School 21, provides a framework through which we can understand what constitutes good speaking in different contexts. It breaks the skills within oracy down into four distinct but interlinked strands: physical, linguistic, cognitive, and social and emotional.

THE PHYSICAL STRAND

When watching a speaker, it tends to be the physical aspects of their delivery that we notice first. The physical strand encompasses all of the physical elements of speaking and listening: your body language, gestures, eye contact, facial expressions, and clarity of pronunciation and how you vary the tone, pitch, pace, and volume of your voice.

It can be useful to think about the physical aspects of your voice as you would an instrument, which can be practiced and altered. Just as you would

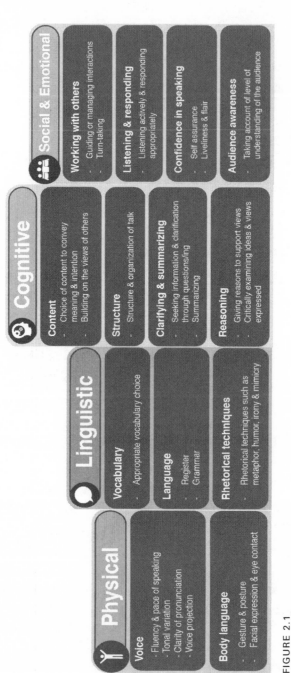

FIGURE 2.1
The Oracy Framework
Voice 21

become more skillful in playing an instrument, with good teaching and plenty of practice, students can become more skillful in how they use their voices. For instance, when telling a story, students can learn to vary the tone and volume of their voice to build suspense; when speaking in a small group, some students may need to be taught to speak at an appropriate volume.

THE LINGUISTIC STRAND

To communicate effectively, we rely on language. The linguistic strand relates to the words that we choose to use and how we bring these together through speech. Essentially, it means knowing which words and phrases to use and when to use them in order to convey ideas effectively.

Vocabulary choices can require us to be very subject specific and specialist. In order to describe a process in science such as photosynthesis, for example, students must be able to understand and use scientific words such as *chloroplasts*, *chlorophyll*, and *glucose*.

In other situations—for example, when telling a story—students might choose to use emotive or descriptive language. This could be through the use of rhetorical devices: using a simile or metaphor to add depth to a description, or employing exaggeration or irony for effect. Both of these examples illustrate the significance of our language choices in different contexts.

Another important aspect of the linguistic strand is being able to adapt the way we speak according to the level of formality required in a given situation. In order to change their register, students must understand how to adapt their speech, for example, when chatting with friends or addressing an important visitor.

THE COGNITIVE STRAND

The cognitive strand describes the thought processes that underpin speaking and listening. You cannot separate the skills of speaking from the content of what is being said. Someone can be an amazing performer, but if what they are saying makes no sense or lacks a basis in reasoning, then they cannot be a good speaker.

The ability to formulate relevant ideas and develop reasoning are key cognitive skills. Students need to be able to organize and structure their thoughts and at times summarize or prioritize information. As well as articulating their

BOX 2.1

ORACY IN ACTION: TEACHING THE ORACY FRAMEWORK

When introducing the Oracy Framework to students or colleagues, it is useful to isolate each of the strands in order to develop a deeper understanding of each component of good talk. A fun way to do this is by playing four games, one to exemplify each of the strands.

1. WHAT'S THE WORD?

Strand: *Linguistic*

This game is played in groups of three to six students. Provide each group with a number of word cards. These could feature objects, such as a map or an airplane. A more challenging selection could feature concepts, such as freedom or democracy. A player must describe what is on the card to teammates without saying the actual word and without using gestures or actions.

Variations of this game could include subject-specific or technical vocabulary that you would like students to learn—for example, key scientific or mathematical vocabulary.

To be successful in this activity, students must reach for alternative vocabulary in order to describe the word on the card.

2. THE 1–20 GAME

Strand: *Social and emotional*

Sit your students in one large circle. Explain that, as a group, you are going to count from one to twenty. However, you cannot simply go around the circle in order, taking turns to say a number. You must start by saying *one*; a student must then jump in and say *two*, another *three*. If two people speak at the same time, the group must begin again at one.

To be successful at this game, students must "read the room," using eye contact to establish whether it is the right time to speak. It is worth playing this game a number of times and recording the highest number you reach. Try to beat this each time you play! This is a great game to start a talk-focused lesson, as it ensures everybody is engaged and on task.

This game is about group dynamics; students must be aware of others and wait patiently for an opportunity to speak.

3. WHICH EMOTION?

Strand: *Physical*

Provide students with a statement, such as "It's going to snow today" and a number of different emotions, such as excited, disappointed, nervous, ecstatic, confused, worried, and angry. In groups, students must say the statement as if they are feeling one of the emotions you have provided. The rest of their group must guess which emotion they were feeling.

In order to express which emotion they are feeling, students have to manipulate their voice, consciously adapting their tone and changing their facial expressions and adding actions.

4. IF I RULED THE WORLD . . .

Strand: *Cognitive*

This game is an adaptation of a popular game show from the 1990s. Students play in groups of four to six. One player begins by saying, "If I ruled the world, I would . . . because . . ." and describing what they would do and why. For example, the first student might say, "If I ruled the world I would make the working week four days long because it would improve worker morale." The next person must say, "I couldn't disagree more because . . ." and explain why they disagree (even if they don't!). For example, a responder might say, "I couldn't disagree more because if the working week was four days long the economy would suffer." They must then state what they would do if they ruled the world, the next person must disagree, and so on.

This game requires students to use logic and reason, providing explanations for why they disagree and proposing new ideas.

own thinking, the cognitive strand requires students to be able to explore others' reasoning by engaging with different points of view and asking questions.

THE SOCIAL AND EMOTIONAL STRAND

Fundamentally, speaking is a social activity. Although on occasion we may talk to ourselves, most speaking tends to be in the form of dialogue with others or to an audience. The social and emotional strand relates to our confidence and interactions with others: how we conduct ourselves within a group, present ourselves to an audience, and listen effectively to others.

Judging the balance between sharing ideas and allowing enough time and space for others to share theirs during group discussion is an important social and emotional skill. Similarly, listening closely to what others are saying and responding appropriately in a group situation, as well as reading the mood of a room when speaking to an audience, all require social and emotional awareness.

A range of ideas to introduce the Oracy Framework to students or colleagues is outlined in Box 2.1.

TYPES OF TALK

The oracy skills set out under the four strands of the Oracy Framework differ according to the context in which someone is speaking. The oracy skills required to solve a problem in the workplace, make a complaint, comfort a child, or speak to an audience, for example, are all very different.

Similarly, in the classroom, there are a number of different contexts in which students will develop their oracy skills, each of which requires a different skillset. For example, the skills required for students to speak at length in front of their classmates are distinct from those required to work cooperatively in order to share and develop ideas with their peers.

To help conceptualize and understand the differences between the types of talk that most commonly happen in the classroom, Douglas Barnes has made a distinction between exploratory and presentational types of talk.

Exploratory talk describes how we develop and explore ideas together. According to Barnes, exploratory talk is "typical of the early stages of approaching new ideas . . . Exploratory talk is hesitant and incomplete because it enables the speaker to try out ideas, to hear how they sound, to see what others make of them, to arrange information and ideas into different patterns."[2]

BOX 2.2

ORACY IN ACTION: WHAT TYPE OF TALK IS HAPPENING IN YOUR CLASSROOM?

Observe the typical talk taking place in your classroom. What do you notice or hear when your students are discussing a question or problem in small groups? It may be worth looking out for:

- How they position themselves in groups
- How they use their tone of voice and body language
- The balance of talk among individuals in the group
- The types of contributions being made: do students build on, challenge, or question what others have said?
- Whether they are able to reach agreement as a group

Broadly, group talk in the classroom falls into three categories (Mercer 2008).[1] Which type of talk do you think is closest to what you observed your students engaging in?

CUMULATIVE TALK

- Contributions build on each other but go unchallenged.
- Ideas may be repeated or elaborated upon.
- Contributions are accepting and uncritical rather than questioning or challenging.

You might hear:

- "Yes, also . . ."
- "Yes, it's like what X said . . ."
- "That's probably right."

This type of talk might look harmonious, and therefore at first glance be mistaken for being productive. However, it risks students internalizing misconceptions and failing to engage with other points of view (they lack anyone playing devil's advocate). Their readiness to agree with each other may also foreclose them opening up new lines of inquiry, engaging with different ways of thinking, or considering challenging perspectives.

DISPUTATIONAL TALK

- There is frequent disagreement, which may not be supported with reasons.
- Contributions are competitive rather than collaborative.
- Nobody bridges the gap between different ideas and opinions.
- Students hold on to their own views.

You might hear:

○ "Yes, it is."/"No, it isn't."

○ "No, that's not right, it's . . ."

○ "Anyway, back to what I said . . ."

Disputational talk treads the fine line between being a waste of time and becoming a full-blown argument. Students gain little from it, as they are only engaging with others' opinions at a surface level, if at all. As a result of their unwillingness to concede ground to each other, they fail to use their collective thinking power to work toward a common goal or understanding.

EXPLORATORY TALK

- There is a sense of collaboration and shared purpose. This could be trying to reach a shared agreement or solve a problem.
- Contributions are treated with respect.
- Students offer reasons for their opinions.
- Students are not afraid to politely challenge, question, or probe each other's ideas.

You might hear:

- "To challenge what you said . . ."
- "Do you mean . . ."
- "How about . . ."
- "Linking to what X said . . ."
- "Is it like when . . ."

Exploratory talk is messy talk, where students grapple with meaning and make it their own. This is the most desirable type of group talk; it is educationally productive, helping students to develop their understanding and move their learning forward.

NOTE

1. N. Mercer, "Three Kinds of Talk," University of Cambridge Resources for Teachers, 2008, https://thinkingtogether.educ.cam.ac.uk/resources/5_examples_of_talk_in_groups.pdf. Accessed April 12, 2018.

During exploratory talk, students listen to each other's ideas, interacting and engaging critically with them. New thoughts or ideas might be suggested or proposed as a result of what someone else has said and misconceptions do not go unchallenged. Students give reasons for or explanations of their ideas or challenges and group members work toward building consensus or shared understanding of the idea or problem at hand. It is through this kind of talk that students develop their conceptual understanding and take ownership of their own learning.

Your students will not necessarily know how to engage in exploratory talk. It can be useful to observe the talk already happening in your classroom, as suggested in Box 2.2. Taking the time to step back and listen to how your students use talk to support their learning currently will help you to build on these skills and support you to develop a culture of exploratory talk in your classroom.

In contrast, presentational talk involves students "presenting" their understanding to others. This does not mean that all presentational talk involves delivery of prepared material to an audience but rather that the focus of the talk has shifted from the individual to the audience. As Barnes explains, "in presentational talk the speaker's attention is primarily focused on adjusting the language, content and manner to the needs of the audience, and in exploratory talk the speaker is more concerned with sorting out his or her own thoughts."[3]

Contexts for Exploratory Talk

- Solving a problem collaboratively
- Discussing an issue
- Explaining or interpreting a diagram with a group
- Engaging in role play

Contexts for Presentational Talk

- Participating in a formal debate
- Hosting an event
- Giving a presentation
- Answering a teacher's question (when the focus is on sharing rather than developing understanding)

EXPECTATIONS FOR TALK

When planning for talk in the classroom, it is important to know whether you are asking students to engage in presentational or exploratory talk, as your expectations and the way you set up a task will be different depending on which type of talk you request of students.

It is also worth considering where each type of talk falls within a sequence of learning. As Barnes notes, presentational talk is more appropriate toward the end of a sequence of learning, when pupils have already had plenty of opportunities to develop and refine their understanding through exploratory talk.[4]

Once you have decided which type of talk is appropriate for a given learning outcome, it is a good idea to develop a set of success criteria for the talk components of the task at hand and share these with pupils. The four strands

Table 2.1.

	Exploratory Talk *A small-group discussion on a recently conducted science experiment*	Presentational Talk *A presentation on the findings from a science experiment*
Physical	• Students face each other and demonstrate open body language. • Volume and tone of voice appropriate to small-group discussion. • Students give eye contact to the person speaking.	• Students project their voices, speaking loudly and clearly so that everyone can hear. • Students adopt an appropriate posture, using gestures where appropriate to support the delivery of their ideas.
Linguistic	• Students use appropriate scientific vocabulary.	• Students include appropriate scientific vocabulary in their presentations, explaining this when necessary. • Students adopt a formal register.
Cognitive	• Students give reasons to support their views, referring to the outcome of the experiment, or their own prior experiences, where appropriate. • Students clarify each other's contributions and seek further information through questioning. • Students build or elaborate on each other's ideas and offer a challenge where appropriate.	• The presentation is structured clearly and appropriately, including an introduction and conclusion as well as explanation of key ideas. • The information included is relevant and clearly explained.
Social and Emotional	• Students ensure that everybody has a chance to speak, inviting contributions from those that have not yet done so. • Students listen carefully to each other's contributions.	• The content of the presentation is adapted appropriately for the audience. • The students' delivery is confident and self-assured.

of the Oracy Framework provide a useful lens through which to do this. Table 2.1 provides an example of the different success criteria that might be expected for an exploratory and presentational task in the science classroom.

The setup and scaffolding provided for each of the tasks outlined in table 2.1 would be very different. To encourage students to use evidence to support their ideas or to include scientific vocabulary when discussing the outcome of an experiment, you could provide students with a table of results or key scientific vocabulary cards. You may also wish to talk to your students about the conventions of discussion—how to ensure everyone has a turn to speak, for example—before setting them off on this task.

In contrast, the setup and scaffolding provided for the presentational task would be very different. You may, for example, choose to set aside time to work on the physical aspects of the presentation's delivery, perhaps working on your students' voice projection or posture. You may also spend some time talking to students about their audience and encouraging them to consider how to adapt the content of their presentations accordingly. The content of a presentation explaining an idea to scientists would be very different to one explaining a similar idea or concept to younger students.

To support your students to become great speakers, it is essential to understand the skills required for good oracy and how these differ depending on the context in which someone is speaking. The Oracy Framework provides a way of breaking down these skills depending on the context—exploratory or presentational—in which a student is speaking. It is important that you make your expectations for each of the four strands clear and explicitly teach the skills your students need to work on. How to teach the discussion skills required to engage in exploratory talk is the focus of the next chapter.

QUESTIONS TO CONSIDER

- Which elements of the four strands are your students' strengths and weaknesses?
- How do you support your students to develop each of the four strands?
- What is the balance of exploratory and presentational talk in your classroom?
- How do you share your expectations for different types of talk with your students?

NOTES

1. B. Maxwell, C. Burnett, J. Reidy, B. Willis, and S. Demack, *Oracy Curriculum, Culture and Assessment Toolkit: Evaluation Report and Executive Summary* (London: Education Endowment Foundation, 2015).

2. D. Barnes, "Exploratory Talk for Learning," in *Exploring Talk in School Inspired by the Work of Douglas Barnes*, eds. Neil Mercer and Steve Hodgkinson (London: SAGE Publications, 2008), 5.

3. Ibid.

4. Ibid., 5.

3

Deconstruct and Teach Discussion

Discussion, the most common form of exploratory talk, is a powerful tool for learning. In a discussion, students share their ideas and engage with those of others. Instead of passively receiving information, students are actively involved in the development of their own knowledge and understanding. In a successful discussion, students constantly reevaluate their own position in relation to others' and, crucially, learn from their peers, not just the teacher.

Discussions require students to work hard and apply themselves; following and contributing to the thread of a well-thought-out discussion is cognitively demanding. What's more, in a discussion, students are accountable to their peers, not just themselves or the teacher, which means there are higher levels of engagement than during individual classroom pursuits.

If discussion leads to such good learning, why do we not see it more regularly in the classroom? The answer is twofold. First, discussion requires a shift in our understanding of the role of the teacher; during a student-led discussion, the teacher is a facilitator, rather than an imparter of knowledge, creating opportunities for pupils to develop and rehearse their understanding together. Second, and perhaps most important, a discussion requires a degree of trust between a teacher and their students; the teacher cannot listen in to every discussion and so they must trust that student discussion is focused and productive.

To ensure that classroom discussions are productive, providing students with opportunities to develop and refine their understanding, pupils must be taught *how* to have a discussion. Your students might not have a frame of reference for a good discussion, having not had the opportunity to practice these skills at home. Moreover, most models of discourse found on the TV tend to be disputational; politicians or contestants on gameshows rarely sit down together and discuss their ideas politely and respectfully.

GROUND RULES FOR DISCUSSION

We cannot assume that students know the hallmarks of an effective discussion or that they will "work them out" without explicit teaching. In fact, some students may enter into a discussion with their own unhelpful preconceptions, such as "It's rude to disagree with someone."

To support pupils to understand what makes effective discussion and create positive norms for talk, academics working on the Thinking Together project at Cambridge University have advocated for creating a set of ground rules for talk.[1] Once created, these should serve as a set of success criteria for effective discussion and should be referred back to regularly, both when setting up and when evaluating student discussion.

Ground rules for talk or discussion guidelines could include:

1. Always respect each other's ideas.
2. Invite others to contribute.
3. Demonstrate active listening.
4. Be prepared to change your mind.
5. Try to come to a shared agreement.

Ground rules for talk are most powerful when co-created with students. However, most students are unlikely to be able to make appropriate suggestions if they have had little prior experience of group talk.

Film Clips

A great way to support pupils to generate ground rules for talk is to share film clips of discussions. Although sharing excellent examples of discussions is beneficial, sharing examples of less successful discussions can be more powerful. Students tend to find it easier to pick out negative behaviors rather than identifying exactly why a particular discussion was so successful. Excellent examples of terrible discussions are bountiful in TV shows such as *The Apprentice*!

A lighthearted and fun alternative is to film a group of teachers having a disastrous discussion (giving one-word answers, staring at the ceiling, fidgeting, muttering, going off topic, dominating the discussion, or ignoring others) and ask students to pick out what it is they are doing wrong!

Once students have had the opportunity to reflect on why your discussion did not go so well and you have elicited these ideas from them, it is time to reframe these negative observations as positives, which can serve as components of your class's ground rules:

"You were looking out the window," for example, might become "We always look at the person who is speaking." "You laughed at what he was saying" could become "We always treat each other's ideas with respect."

Creating a class set of ground rules for talk or discussion guidelines is only the first step in teaching students how to have an effective discussion. Once these rules have been written, it is important that they are prominently displayed and regularly referred to, both before and after each discussion you have. Your students should know them inside out!

In Box 3.1 and Box 3.2 you can read more about different discussion guidelines you might want to focus on with your students and how to teach these.

DISCUSSION ROLES

Once you have taught your students the ground rules for good discussion, it is important to spend some time teaching them about the types of contributions they can make in a discussion. This will help ensure that discussions develop their thinking, reasoning, and understanding.

The most important thing for students to understand is that each contribution to a discussion should link to what has been said previously. This moves group talk away from a simple sharing of ideas and toward a collaborative learning exercise.

A great way to do this is by creating a visual representation of a discussion, using a ball of string. Provide the "instigator," the student who starts off the conversation, with a ball of string. They must hold on to the end and pass the ball to the next person who speaks, who holds on to their section of string before passing the ball to the next speaker. At the end of the discussion, students will have a visual representation of who spoke when in the discussion,

BOX 3.1

PRAISE FOR CHANGING YOUR MIND

When working with my class of eight- and nine-year-olds, I noticed that lots of students thought that a discussion could be "won" if everybody thought the same thing as them by the end. To help students understand that the purpose of a discussion is to share their ideas and learn from each other, I explicitly praised those children who had changed their mind during a discussion.

This involved talking to students explicitly about changing their mind as a result of what they'd heard:

- "That's great! You thought X at the beginning of your discussion, now you think Y."
- "Who changed their mind during their discussions today?"
- "Can anyone share an idea that made them change their opinion?"

This helped students understand that the purpose of group talk is to listen to each other's ideas and, as a consequence, refine their own thinking, rather than to stubbornly hold on to their own views. As a result, there was a shift in my classroom culture; changing your mind was not seen as a failure, but was instead celebrated. This meant students were less afraid to share their initial ideas on a topic, even if these were not yet fully formed or turned out to be incorrect.

—Amy Gaunt

highlighting the idea that effective discussion involves linking to what has been said previously, following the literal thread of the conversation.

When students understand that discussion goes beyond simply sharing their own ideas, and that they must interact with those of others, it is time to introduce them to discussion roles, as illustrated in figure 3.1. Discussion

BOX 3.2

ORACY IN ACTION: CONSENSUS CIRCLE

The idea that students should work toward reaching consensus, or shared agreement, is an important element of exploratory talk. By requiring students to come to consensus, you are challenging them to synthesize and evaluate their group's thinking, which moves their discussion beyond a simple sharing of ideas.

To do this effectively, students must be taught explicitly what it means to reach a shared agreement and how to get there: looking out for commonalities and comparing ideas, negotiating and being willing to make concessions, weighing evidence, changing their opinion.

A great way to teach students this skill is to use a consensus circle. Split the class into small groups (whatever size group works for you, but bear in mind that it's more difficult for a larger group to reach consensus!) and provide them with a large sheet of paper with a circle drawn on it and a pack of sticky notes. Explain to students that the circle on the paper is a magical "consensus circle" and the only ideas that can go in there are ones with which everybody in the group agrees.

Now provide students with a question that engenders multiple and varied responses. In English, this could be "What is the most powerful word in the poem?" In history, "What were the most significant causes of X event?"

Give pupils some time to generate ideas alone, writing one on each sticky note. Next, ask students to spread out their ideas around the outside of the circle. They must decide as a group which ideas to put inside the consensus circle. Provide students with a maximum number of ideas that can go into the circle. Three or four works well. Ensure students understand that they must try to reach agreement through listening to each other, trading off ideas, and negotiating.

Instigator

Starts the discussion or
opens up a new topic for
discussion

———————

I would like to start by saying...
I think we should consider...

Builder

Develops, adds to or
runs with an idea

———————

I agree, and I would like to add...
Building on that idea,
I think...

Challenger

Gives reasons to disagree or
presents an alternative
argument

———————

I disagree with you because...
You mentioned X but
what about...

Clarifier

Simplifies and makes
things clearer by asking
questions

———————

What do you mean when you
say...?
Does that mean...?

Prober

Digs deeper into the
argument, asks for evidence
or justification of ideas

———————

Can you provide an example to
support what you're saying...?
Why do you think...?

Summarizer

Identifies the main ideas
from the discussion.

———————

Overall, the main points were...
Our discussion focused on...

FIGURE 3.1
Discussion Roles
Voice 21

roles set out the types of contributions, or "talk moves," that students can play in a discussion. There are six roles: instigator, builder, challenger, clarifier, prober, and summarizer.

Discussion roles set out specific ways that students can interact with each other's ideas, exercising higher-order thinking skills and in turn raising the quality of talk. Each of the roles breaks down a different skill set out in the cognitive strand of the Oracy Framework. In a rich discussion, students will play a number of different roles, depending on the content and direction of the discussion, rather than simply sticking to one.

As with most oracy skills, it is important to explicitly teach students how to play each role during a discussion. It's also not advisable to introduce students to all of the roles at once. Instead, introduce one or two roles at a time, depending on the age of your students, and introduce more when they are ready. It is a good idea to prominently display the roles you are working on or even print them as postcards for students to refer to during their discussions.

Instigator

The instigator is the person who starts off a discussion, offering the first contribution. It can also be someone who begins a new line of inquiry, perhaps to move a discussion forward or in a different direction. This is a fairly easy role to teach, particularly when the definition of instigator is limited to the person who makes the first contribution. It is, however, worth spending some time teaching students that, when their discussion has reached an impasse, introducing a new idea or changing the direction of discussion is an effective way of moving the discussion forward.

Builder

The builder develops an idea, elaborating on what someone else has said, adding more detail, or giving a reason why they agree with somebody else's contribution. It is an excellent role to introduce to students early on, as it reinforces the idea that each contribution to a discussion should link to what has been said previously. With younger students, it can be useful to introduce them to hand gestures to further develop their understanding of the role, building a tower with their fists when saying, "Building on X's idea . . ." or interlacing their fingers when saying, "Linking to X's idea . . ." for example.

Challenger

The challenger disagrees with an idea or presents an alternative argument. It is important to create a classroom culture in which challenge is both valued and encouraged; however, this is not easy to achieve, as students often find it difficult to accept when others disagree with them. It is worth addressing this head-on and explaining to students that it's acceptable to disagree and that, when others challenge our thinking, it can help us see something differently and, in turn, broaden our own understanding.

Disagreeing politely with what somebody else has said is another key teaching point. This can be done by providing students with sentence stems to offer polite challenge, such as "I can see what you're saying; however . . ." or "That's a really interesting idea, but have you considered . . ." It is also worth talking to students about how the tone of voice they use when challenging someone can affect how this is received.

Clarifier

The clarifier's job is to make things clearer by asking questions that encourage others to elucidate their thinking. This could entail asking someone to explain the meaning of a word or concept or checking whether their interpretation of what has been said is correct. The clarifier plays an important role, as they ensure that what is being said is clear to everybody else in the group. A skillful clarifying question can also prompt a speaker to reevaluate their own thinking.

Prober

The prober also asks questions, but these questions dig deeper into an argument, asking for evidence or justification of ideas. The prober ensures that the discussion is accountable to evidence and reason. They may ask a speaker to explain their reasoning or to give evidence for an idea or viewpoint that has been presented.

Summarizer

The summarizer brings together the main threads of a discussion, offering a succinct and balanced evaluation of the ideas presented. Most summaries tend to happen after a discussion has finished; however, it is worth teaching students that the summarizer can also play a useful role during discussion, summarizing what has been said up to that point in order to move the group's thinking forward.

Once your students are familiar with all or some of these discussion roles, add them to your ground rules for talk. For example, "We build on, clarify, and politely challenge each other's ideas."

TIMING

Having deconstructed what makes a great discussion and begun to teach your students these skills, it is important that students have time to put them into practice. How you build up toward extended discussion tasks requires careful consideration. An entire lesson spent on discussion is quite demanding. (Think about how you feel after a long meeting!) Purposeful classroom talk is "work," and it requires skill to sustain it for extended periods.

Teacher judgment over the time given to discussions is crucial, as some discussions will require less time than others and, to ensure that this type of learning remains both engaging and productive, it is worth mixing up opportunities for shorter and more extended discussion tasks.

Discussion need not take up a whole lesson until you and your students are ready for it, or indeed at all, if it doesn't support the learning you want to happen. If talk tasks are new to your students, you might want to start by establishing norms with shorter (one- to two-minute) discussion tasks, extending these when your students are ready. In fact, you will probably notice that, as students master the discussion skills outlined in this chapter, their discussions will naturally run for longer.

That said, judging exactly how long to leave a discussion running can be difficult and will vary depending on the students in the group. On the one hand, you don't want students to run out of things to say too quickly and end up using your lesson time for off-task chatter. However, if students aren't given enough time, they can end up feeling frustrated, especially if they feel they have been cut off midway through an interesting discussion.

Bear in mind that often it can take a little while for a discussion to get going and become truly interesting, as this normally requires everyone to have shared their view and for points of contention to have emerged. There isn't a magic rule of thumb as to how long this takes to happen, but the easiest way to get a sense of how long is needed is to listen in on your students' discussions.

If you feel that they haven't yet touched upon the central argument, you may want to pause the whole class and introduce a subsidiary question to nudge their discussions in the right direction. For example, in a discussion on whether or not to lower the voting age, you might find that your students neglect to talk about the privileges that are already granted to sixteen- or seventeen-year-olds, such as driving, joining the army, or getting married. It may therefore be useful to prompt them to consider this.

There is always a worry that different groups will finish their discussions at different times. One way to manage this is to set up several layers within a task. Rather than providing one discussion question or talking point, give three or five that have different foci and levels of difficulty. Let students choose to discuss the one that interests them most and move on to another when they have finished.

It's also helpful to encourage your students to organize their own time and think metacognitively: Where should the discussion be at the halfway point, at three-quarters through, and by the end? What kinds of things need to be said to make that happen? What might stop a discussion from moving forward? How can you help it to move forward?

You might want to work with your students to develop some useful phrases for supporting time management, such as:

- "We're about halfway through our time. Who hasn't had a chance to speak yet?"
- "We only have X minutes left. Can someone summarize the main points so far?"
- "It seems that we all agree on . . . so shall we move on to talk about . . . ?"
- "It feels like we are stuck on . . . Shall we put it to one side for a moment and talk about . . . instead?"
- "We need to start narrowing down our options. Do we all agree that option A and option B are the best two?"
- "The main issue we haven't yet resolved is . . . But can we all agree that . . . ?"

Alternatively, you can scaffold your students' time more tightly by breaking it into chunks. For instance, when solving a problem through discussion, you could ask them to spend:

- Two minutes discussing the problem. What is the problem? What do we already know about it?
- Two minutes offering as many solutions as possible, without passing judgment. All ideas are good ideas at this point!
- Two minutes evaluating potential solutions. Are there any problems associated with them? Why is one better than another?
- Two minutes reaching consensus on a final course of action. What does everyone in the group think is the best solution?

Through teaching your students discussion skills, you will build their stamina and independence, gradually enabling them up to speak for more extended periods of time.

THE TEACHER'S ROLE IN DISCUSSION

In order to become experts in exploratory talk, students should be given plenty of opportunities to practice without too much interference from the teacher. What then is your role during whole-class or small-group discussion?

During whole-class discussion you have a chance to model different types of contributions and encourage your students to take on different roles (for example, "Would anyone like to challenge X's idea?" or "Can anyone summarize X's perspective?").

However, be aware that your presence in a discussion can alter the dynamics, as students are often tempted to filter their responses through you, instead of speaking directly to each other. Instead, try to break your class into smaller groups where there will be more opportunities for students to speak and put their emerging discussion skills into practice.

Once your students have settled into their discussion groups, try to circulate, listening in unobtrusively to different groups' discussions. If a student shares a misconception with their group, it is tempting to jump in and address this immediately. However, it is worth waiting to see if someone else in the group does this for you. Breaking down a misconception as part of group talk is a powerful way for students to develop both their reasoning and their understanding. If a misconception still goes unchallenged, you can address this with the whole class once their discussions have finished.

When student discussions draw to an end, it is important that students are not always asked to summarize their discussions through whole-class feedback for the benefit of the teacher; this gives the impression that student-to-teacher talk is more important than student-to-student talk. Instead, this is the perfect occasion for you to summarize the class's discussions or to share an interesting idea you heard while circulating.

Shifting the balance of talk away from you as a teacher and toward your students can heighten some of our "greatest vulnerabilities: classroom control and subject knowledge," as Robin Alexander notes.[2] It is inevitable that in devolving talk to groups of students you will have less control over the direction of the lesson. However, this isn't something to fear. By teaching your students the skills to engage in productive discussion, you are enabling them to drive forward their own learning.

However, teaching discussion skills alone is not enough. It is also important to carefully consider what it is your students are talking about. In order for talk to stimulate genuine thinking, new ideas, and connections, students must also feel invested in the topic and that they have something to say.

QUESTIONS TO CONSIDER

- Do your students know the ingredients of a great discussion?
- How can you teach your students to have an effective discussion?
- What is your role while your students are taking part in independent group discussion?

NOTES

1. L. Dawes, N. Mercer, and R. Wegerif, *Thinking Together: A Programme of Activities for Developing Speaking, Listening and Thinking Skills for Children Aged 8–11* (Birmingham, England: Imaginative Minds, 2000), 3.

2. R. Alexander, "Improving Oracy and Classroom Talk in English Schools: Achievements and Challenges" (presented at Department for Education seminar on oracy, February 20, 2012), 6, http://www.robinalexander.org.uk/wp-content/uploads/2012/06/DfE-oracy-120220-Alexander-FINAL.pdf.

4

Remember, You Can't Talk about Nothing

An interesting and thought-provoking discussion is reliant upon those participating in the discussion having something to say. It is thus a teacher's responsibility not only to teach students *how* to have successful discussions, but to design purposeful, engaging tasks that get students talking and that support the learning goals of a lesson. It is therefore important to consider *what* you are asking your students to talk about. This chapter will outline three key considerations when choosing a stimulus for talk: purpose, outcome, and student motivation.

PURPOSE

The most important thing to consider when designing a talk task is what the purpose for talk is and how this links to the projected sequence of learning. Possible purposes for talk in your classroom could include to gauge understanding or prior knowledge, to unearth misconceptions, to apply knowledge in a new context, to practice new vocabulary, or to evaluate and compare ideas.

The purpose for talk may also change depending on where in a sequence of learning the talk takes place. For example, in a science classroom where students are learning why there is day and night, the purpose for talk at the start of a sequence of learning is likely to be to gauge students' prior knowledge and unearth misconceptions, which can be addressed later on.

Toward the end of the sequence of learning, the purpose for talk may shift, as pupils have developed their knowledge and understanding. The purpose for talk in this context might be to apply their newfound understanding in a different context or to ask questions to further their understanding. In this particular example, students could apply their knowledge in a new context, working together to explain why people in Alaska experience "midnight sun."

It is important, therefore, that the stimulus for talk you identify suits the purpose you have in mind. Concept cartoons, outlined in Box 4.1, are an excellent way of supporting students to deepen their understanding and apply their knowledge in a new context.

Stimuli for talk can also be created to support students to acquire new knowledge through talking together. To do this, the teacher must carefully consider how to feed the appropriate subject content into student discussions and how students will engage with this material. Boxes 4.2 and 4.3 explore two strategies you can use to develop subject knowledge through talk.

BOX 4.1

ORACY IN ACTION: CONCEPT CARTOONS

Concept cartoons were developed by Brenda Keogh and Stuart Naylor.[1] They feature a range of characters putting forward different ideas or opinions on a given subject. The cartoons were originally intended for use in science education and feature characters trying to explain a scientific concept or occurrence in order to provoke discussion and stimulate scientific thinking. The cartoons often contain common scientific misconceptions and prompt students to address these through talk, providing an ideal way for students to apply their knowledge and develop their understanding together.

Even when provided with a carefully constructed question or talking point, some students may find it hard to begin a discussion. For some students, putting their own ideas out for discussion can be very daunting. A concept cartoon, which offers a group of fictional characters' ideas up for consideration, is an excellent way into discussion for students who may be wary of voicing their own opinions, but who may feel less daunted analyzing the views of others.

Although originally developed for science, concept cartoons are an excellent springboard for talk in any subject. To create your own concept cartoon, come up with a statement or question relating to the topic you are studying—for example, "Does the Iron Man deserve to be punished?" in English. Then have a number of characters respond, each with a speech bubble explaining what they think about this question. Be sure to include some controversial ideas or misconceptions. Students can then apply their own knowledge, in this case of the book *The Iron Man*,[2] to explain who they agree with and why.

When using a concept cartoon as a stimulus for group discussion, begin by asking pupils to decide who they agree with the most and least. Students may also wish to decide why a particular character holds a certain viewpoint or to explain how they might have picked up a stated misconception. Then encourage students to use the characters' ideas to develop their own response to the question. An example of a concept cartoon exploring the difference between discussion and debate is included in figure 4.1.

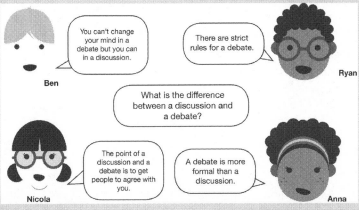

FIGURE 4.1
Concept Cartoon

NOTES

1. S. Naylor and B. Keogh, *Concept Cartoons in Science Education* (London: Millgate House, 2000).

2. T. Hughes, *The Iron Man* (London: Faber and Faber, 1968).

BOX 4.2

ORACY IN ACTION: FED-IN FACTS

Provide students with a stimulus, such as a photograph or historical artifact, and a question to answer through discussion, such as "What is it?" or "What does this show?" While students are talking, feed facts into the group at regular intervals in order to guide and enrich their discussions. If a historical artifact is used, the facts could, for example, provide more information on what the artifact was used for, what time period it is from, or who may have used it.

The stimulus could be a diagram, photograph, audio clip, song, video, word, written passage, or mathematical formula—almost anything! The driving question will vary depending on the stimulus but could be "What's the science here?" as students deconstruct a process diagram or "What's the meaning?" when presenting students with a new or difficult word.

Facts can be fed into the discussion on slips of paper, in numbered envelopes for students to open at their own pace, or by using the "animate" feature on a slide show and having the facts "fly in" at intervals.

Before beginning this activity, it is important that pupils establish how they will work together effectively as a group. How will they share responsibility for reading new facts to the group? How will they ensure everybody has a chance to contribute and that all opinions are heard?

This activity is a great way to drip-feed knowledge into a discussion while giving students ownership over the discovery process.

NOTES

1. This strategy was developed by Anna Kyrk at School 21.

BOX 4.3

ORACY IN ACTION: WHAT'S THE STORY?

Split your students into groups of three to six. Provide each group with a diagram or sequence of images and ask them to explain what is happening—*What's the story?* The images could represent a scientific process, historical event, or character's journey. Students must work together to explain what is happening. This activity could be made more challenging by providing students with a series of unordered images or steps in a process that they have to both decode and put in order.

You may want to provide students with sentence stems and key vocabulary to support their explanations. However, it is worth considering at what stage you introduce key vocabulary; there is merit in allowing students time explore the images and attempt to explain what is happening in their own words before asking them to refine their explanations by incorporating the target vocabulary.

Figure 4.2 is taken from a science classroom where students were trying to explain the concept of natural selection, first using their own words and then rewording their explanations to incorporate eight scientific vocabulary terms: *adaptation, camouflage, genetic, mutation, natural selection, predator, random,* and *variation.*

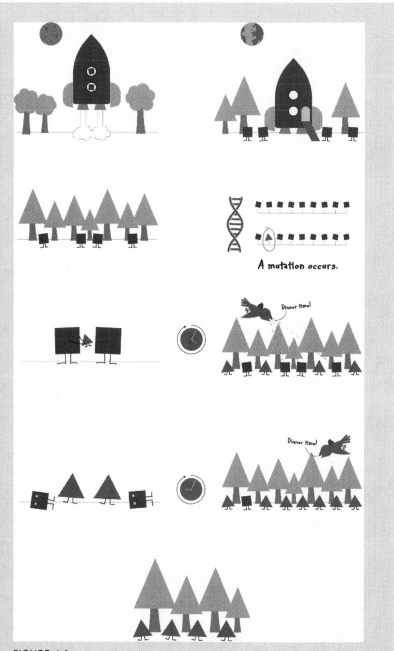

FIGURE 4.2
What's the Story?
Image: Ben Rollo-Hayward

NOTES

1. This strategy was conceived by Anna Kyrk and Henry Ward, teachers at School 21, to support students to develop their understanding of difficult scientific concepts.

OUTCOME

To make certain that student discussions are focused and productive, try to ensure that there is an outcome for talk. Building in a requirement for students to make a decision, reach consensus, or perform some other task as an endpoint for their talk guarantees that discussions stay focused and do not veer off track. It also serves as a record of what has been achieved through student discussion and is a good way to verify whether students remained on task.

An outcome for talk can be something as simple as asking students to come to a decision or reach consensus as a group. Talking points, developed by Lyn Dawes, provide an excellent stimulus for discussion and require students to work toward reaching consensus. Talking points are explored in more detail in Box 4.4.

BOX 4.4

ORACY IN ACTION: TALKING POINTS

Talking points are a set of controversial, thought-provoking, sometimes factually incorrect statements related to a given topic that promote discussion.

When using talking points, students should work toward reaching consensus as a group. This ensures that discussion remains focused and purposeful. It is useful to provide students with sentence stems, such as, "I agree/disagree with the statement because . . ." to begin their discussions. Ultimately, it does not matter if groups are unable to reach consensus; however, setting the expectation that students should work toward developing a shared understanding is important to ensure that talk remains on track.

It can be effective to provide groups of students with a list of talking points about a given topic. Groups can then either work their way through the talking points or choose to discuss the ones that interest them most. As well as providing pupils with choice, this solves the problem of different groups finishing their discussions at different times, as groups can always move on to discuss another talking point if they finish early.

Below are a set of subject-specific talking points. However, for more examples and a far more comprehensive explanation of talking points and how they promote learning, please see Lyn Dawes's excellent book *Talking Points: Discussion Activities in the Primary Classroom.*[1]

Science

- The heavier an object, the faster it will fall.
- Any substance can change state if enough heat energy is applied.
- Trees can breathe.

English

- Edward Tulane is egotistical (a character from *The Miraculous Journey of Edward Tulane*)[2].
- The purpose of a story is to entertain the reader.
- There is no place for flowery prose in nonfiction writing.

Mathematics

- To multiply a number, you just add a zero.
- There is no point learning times tables when you can just use a calculator.
- Fractions: the numerator should always be smaller than the denominator.

NOTES

1. L. Dawes, *Talking Points: Discussion Activities in the Primary Classroom* (Oxon: David Fulton, 2012).

2. K. DiCamillo, *The Miraculous Journey of Edward Tulane* (London: Walker Books, 2008).

A good discussion prompt should provide opportunities for students to share, justify, and defend their ideas, listen to others' perspectives, and, if appropriate, come to consensus. An excellent way to do this is by playing "Which one does not belong?" as outlined in Box 4.5. This is a simple yet effective strategy to generate talk and requires groups of students to make a decision.

BOX 4.5

ORACY IN ACTION: WHICH ONE DOES NOT BELONG?

Provide students with three or four words, images, or objects and ask them to decide which one does not belong. To generate discussion, it is important that any one of the items shared could be the odd one out. In this activity, students must propose ideas, give reasons, and, where appropriate, provide evidence for their theories. They must then listen to others' ideas and choose to agree or to defend their own position. Finally, students must seek to come to a group consensus as to which one does not belong.
Below is a list of subject-specific ideas for this exercise.

HISTORY

Ask students to identify which one does not belong from a number of different figures from a period of history. To engender a number of different possibilities, try to choose figures that have had different experiences, levels of power, or status; have made different decisions; or are perceived differently in the present day. Alternatively, you could give students a number of different primary and secondary sources and also introduce key words, such as *bias* or *reliability*, to help steer student discussion.

ENGLISH

Give students a number of different characters from a book (or different books), a selection of book covers, or a range of settings from books. This is a great way to frame meaningful conversations around books and can be an excellent tool to develop your students' understanding of a book's main characters or themes and to compare different texts or genres. Students should be using evidence from the text to justify their ideas; it is worth setting this as an expectation before students embark on the task.

MATHEMATICS

Supply a selection of numbers: 1, 9, 15, and 8, for example. Younger children may notice that one number has two digits or that one number is even and the rest odd. They may even decide that 1 does not belong because it is made up of only straight, not curved, lines. Older children could decide that 1 is the odd one out because it is the only prime number.

This is an excellent tool for building mathematical vocabulary. A list of target vocabulary for students to use in their explanations could also be provided.

Other ways to use this technique in math could include sharing a range of different fractions, including non-unit fractions; a selection of different shapes, including 2D and 3D shapes; or a set of clocks showing different times.

Providing groups of students with a set of images, objects, or statements to rank according to some given criteria makes available another clear outcome for talk. To support students in this task, it is worth providing them with physical things to rank (pictures, statements printed on strips of paper, etc.)

ORACY IN ACTION: RANKING

Asking students to rank a set of objects, pictures, or statements according to some given criteria is an excellent way to stimulate talk.

HISTORY
Ask students to rank a set of sources according to their reliability. Before beginning, students must mutually agree on a set of criteria for reliability and then evaluate each source accordingly, finally deciding on the order in which the sources should be ranked.

ENGLISH
Provide students with a range of opening sentences or paragraphs from books and ask them to rank them from most compelling to least compelling. To do this, students must first discuss what makes a compelling story opening and judge each sentence or chapter by their criteria. Another idea is to ask students to rank characters from a text they have studied—for instance, who is most culpable for the death of Romeo and Juliet, or which character is most trustworthy?

MATHEMATICS
Give students a range of different examples of how someone has solved a problem with the task of ranking them from most efficient to least efficient. This makes for an interesting discussion about what constitutes an efficient problem-solving method and is a great way to promote talk around a problem in mathematics.

so that they are better able to visualize how they have been ordered. This also allows students to move an image or object tentatively into a different position and seek agreement from their group. A set of subject-specific ideas for ranking are provided in Box 4.6.

Another activity, which is particularly good at generating talk in mathematics and which requires students to come to a decision, is "always, sometimes, never." An explanation of how to use this activity in your classroom can be found in Box 4.7.

BOX 4.7

ORACY IN ACTION:
ALWAYS, SOMETIMES, NEVER

In this activity students are provided with a set of statements and must decide whether they are always true, sometimes true, or never true. In order to do this, students must find examples that prove or disprove a given hypothesis.

This is a particularly effective way of generating talk in mathematics, as it promotes reasoning and encourages students to find examples to support their ideas. It is also a great way for teachers to assess understanding of a given idea or topic before embarking on a unit of work.

Below is a set of example statements that could be used to run this activity in mathematics.

- A square is a rectangle.
- Multiples of 5 always end in 5.
- When you add two odd numbers together you get an even number.
- A quadrilateral has four right angles.
- When you multiply a number it gets bigger.
- Multiples of 10 always end in 0.

STUDENT MOTIVATION

Finally, the best classroom discussions are usually those in which students feel personally invested in the content. It is worth considering how a topic relates to the lives of your students; they are more likely to be engaged, and discussions will therefore be of higher quality, if the content they are discussing is interesting and relevant to them. This isn't to say that you should *only* ask students to discuss subjects they are already interested in, but rather that you should consider how you frame discussion in order to spark lively conversation.

One way to do this is to use "would you rather?" questions. These are explained further in Box 4.8. They can be an entertaining way to make a subject

---

BOX 4.8

ORACY IN ACTION: WOULD YOU RATHER?

"Would you rather?" questions make for an amusing start to a lesson. They are an excellent way to get students talking and rehearsing important talk skills while also having fun. Below are a few silly "Would you rather?" questions that would make a perfect warm-up for a talk-focused lesson.

- Would you rather be a fish or a bird?
- Would you rather live in the year 2300 or 1300?
- Would you rather be poor and happy or rich and unhappy?

Ask students to consider the pros and cons of each choice as a group, ensuring that they provide reasons for their opinions. Encourage students to reach a group decision and justify it to the rest of the class.

Why not ask your students to create their own amusing "would you rather?" questions for the class to discuss? However, don't forget that "would you rather?" questions can also be a great way into a weightier discussion—for example, "Would you rather live under a benevolent dictatorship or in a dysfunctional democracy?"

feel relevant to students, as they have to make a choice that would in theory affect them.

QUESTIONS TO CONSIDER

- What is the purpose for talk and how does this help you to choose an appropriate stimulus?
- Is there an outcome for talk? Do students need to make a decision or reach consensus?
- Is the stimulus for talk relevant to your students' lives? Is it worth talking about?

Structure Oracy

A successful oracy task must be well planned and carefully structured. Students should be in no doubt as to what their role is, who they should be talking to, and for what purpose.

Think of structuring talk as setting up the rules of the game. If you were to ask a group of students to have a soccer match, most would know that they need an equal number of players on each team, one person in goal, and that they can't pick up the ball with their hands! A group with a stronger understanding and higher level of experience in the sport might start allocating players into specific positions: defender, striker, midfielder etc.

This is because they have a very clear understanding of what is expected in a game of soccer, and the boundaries within which the game is to take place. As every player knows the rules of the game, they are freed up to think about what is important: working as a team to win the match. They know the structure of the game, even if they don't yet know how it will unfold once they are on the field.

Well-structured talk functions in the same way. Students need to understand what is expected of them for a specific task. This frees them up to think about *what* they want to say—the ideas in play—rather than the rules they are operating within. Purposeful talk is reliant upon having clear structures in place. This chapter reviews three ways to structure talk in your classroom: via groupings, roles, and protocols.

GROUPINGS

The simplest way to start thinking about organizing talk in your classroom is through using groupings: how many students are working together and how they are arranged to speak with each other.

It can be tempting to use a lot of whole-class discussion, as it enables you to remain in control, monitor what is being said, and assess where your students are in their learning. However, in a class of twenty-five students where only one voice can be heard at a time, whole-class discussion imposes a tight restriction on the length and number of contributions each student can make. It's unlikely that every child will get to speak, let alone be able to speak more than once.

For this reason, try devolving discussion tasks to smaller groups of students. This way, your students will have far more opportunities to speak and you are freed up to listen. You will be able get a much better picture of what your students know and what you need to do to move their understanding forward if you are listening into their discussions rather than directing them.

It is worth having a number of different groupings, as shown in figure 5.1, in your repertoire to ensure that your students have opportunities to talk to a range of different people.

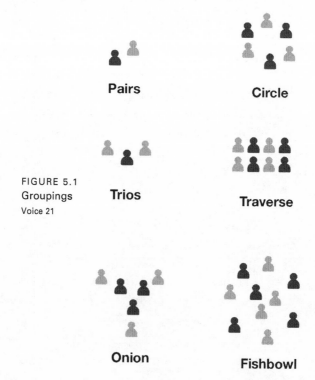

Pairs

Circle

FIGURE 5.1
Groupings   **Trios**
Voice 21

Traverse

Onion

Fishbowl

Pairs

If you are just starting to build a culture of talk in your classroom, pairs are the place to start. Invest time in building strong habits for paired talk: make it normal for students to physically turn to face each other, maintain eye contact, and take turns to speak and listen.

Successful paired talk relies as much upon listening as it does upon speaking. The student listening needs to develop an awareness of their role as an audience: showing active listening, building on their partner's ideas, and asking questions where appropriate.

Some paired talk activities are outlined in Box 5.1.

BOX 5.1

ORACY IN ACTION: PAIRED TALK

QUESTION TENNIS

This helps to generate lots of ideas or questions on a topic, or a stimulus such as a piece of artwork or a photograph. Partner A starts with their question, then Partner B goes, then back to A and so on, like a rally in a game of tennis. If one person hesitates for too long or can't think of what to say on their turn, their partner wins a point. The idea isn't to answer any of the questions, but rather to generate as many questions as possible and in doing so collect interesting ideas to take forward into the rest of the lesson.

For example, when looking at a painting your students might ask questions like: Who painted this? What period is it from? Why did they choose to use this technique? What is the person in the painting thinking? Is this based on real life? How was the artist feeling when they painted this? Is this their best work? Is this painting well-known? And so on.

RECORDER–SOLVER

This works well for problem-solving in mathematics. Partner A is the "recorder" and has the job of recording the solution that Partner B, the "solver," is explaining. This process requires the solver to talk through each step of their thinking process aloud, in a logical order, making edits or changes as they need to.

For example, if the problem was "What is 6x3?" the solver might say something like this: "First draw six groups of three, then add these together to find the total. Six groups of three is equal to 18, so 6x3 is18."

CONVERSATIONS IN ROLE

One student is in role, for instance as a character or figure from history, and their partner asks questions that they answer in role. This encourages students to explore different points of view.

"YES, AND . . ."

This was a strategy adopted by the team at Pixar[1] to reinforce positivity and openness to ideas. Rather than dismissing anyone's idea, members of the team had to respond by saying "Yes, and . . ." and develop it in some way. Creating a rule like this is a good starting point for introducing to students how to build on each other's ideas, and can help to keep discussions positive.

In pairs, ask one student to share an idea and the other to respond with "Yes, and . . ." The first student then builds again and so on.

"YES, BUT . . ."

The complete opposite of "Yes, and . . ." Introducing a rule that one member of a pair can only open their sentences with "Yes, but . . ." requires students to continually think of counterarguments and reasons to disagree!

NOTE

1. S. Krupp and P. Schoemaker, *Winning the Long Game: How Strategic Leaders Shape the Future* (New York: PublicAffairs, 2014).

Trios

In a trio, there are more voices than in a pair and talk is therefore more likely to develop into a full-fledged discussion. However, the group is still small enough to ensure that every student has plenty of opportunity to speak up and have their share of the airtime.

Trios also work well for quieter students. If one student in a pair is reluctant to speak, this can scupper the conversation and make it one-sided. By contrast, in a trio, if one child is reluctant to contribute, the other two students can still engage in a discussion. The quieter child can then listen, and perhaps speak up further into the conversation when they feel ready to and have heard a few ideas. For new language learners, listening to their peers' discussion also provides them with language models.

Traverse

The traverse requires students to be arranged in two parallel lines, stood facing each other, talking to the person opposite them. One student can run down the outside of their line and join on to the end, in doing so bumping everyone up one space to a new talk partner. This means that students get several opportunities to try out their ideas and listen to what their peers are thinking.

The traverse gets children up on their feet, and in doing so makes the task more physical in nature. Students need control of their posture and body to stand strong and firm on the floor. (For younger students it can be useful to put masking tape down on the floor to mark where they need to stand!) Gestures also become more prominent: students are more likely to use them as their hands are freed up, no longer resting on a table or in their lap.

Also, our voices tend to be stronger and more powerful when we stand up—perfect given that students may need to speak up more than they would in a pair discussion to ensure that their traverse partner can hear them.

Grouping students in the traverse particularly lends itself to setting up debate-style discussions, such as "Yes, but . . ." (see Box 5.1). Allocating one line to argue "for" and the other "against" a topic means that the physical layout of the discussion mirrors the conflicting points of view and can encourage students to engage in a back-and-forth between opposing ideas.

The traverse also provides a great opportunity to practice some whole-class call-and-response sentence stems. These should be tailored to match the type of talk you want to take place. For instance, before students launch into a debate, you might announce: "Line A, repeat after me, 'The biggest reason to support this change is . . .' [students repeat]. Now Line B, coming right back at them with, 'I completely disagree with you because . . .' [students repeat]." This is a chance not only to model language but also the expression in your voice and the gestures you use—a bit of finger-wagging could be added with good effect!

Circle

Asking students to work in small circle groups isn't new or groundbreaking, but it's straightforward and simple, *and* it develops a number of oracy skills.

A circle is a democratic shape, with no obvious front or leader; it is collaborative rather than oppositional or adversarial. It therefore lends itself to group discussion, which all participants enter into as equals.

Moreover, sitting in a circle necessitates eye contact and engagement among all the participants in the group. Circle discussions of up to six students also introduce more voices than smaller groupings, and as a result there are more complex group dynamics. Students need to take care to ensure equitable turn-taking and may need to use questions or other prompts to invite quieter members into their discussion; social and emotional skills are paramount to ensure everyone is included.

Having a larger group discussion as a circle also requires a significant level of cognitive skill. If the group members are to reach a shared agreement, not only will they need to engage with a variety of opinions, but they may have to negotiate and compromise with each other—asking questions, making links, and providing reasons in the process.

Onion

The onion groups students in two concentric circles, just like rings in the cross-section of an onion. The inner circle faces outward in order to speak to the outer circle members, who face inward. You can then rotate either circle clockwise or counterclockwise, in doing so switching the pairs in which students are speaking.

Just like the traverse, the onion requires students to be up on their feet and so is more physical. It also means that students engage with lots of different peers, and hopefully different ideas, as their partners rotate. It's worth noting that for the onion to work well, you will need a decent amount of space, especially if you are using it with a whole class!

Fishbowl

A fishbowl is when an inner circle ("the fish") have a discussion that is observed by an outer circle. This means that unlike in the onion—where the two circles are facing each other—students in a fishbowl all face into the middle of the circle. Rather than grouping the whole class as a single fishbowl, it is often better to split students into smaller groups, with six to ten students forming each fishbowl. Some ideas on how to use a fishbowl to support students to reflect on talk are outlined in chapter 10.

ROLES

Roles are a clear way to set up and structure the type of talk you want to take place by ascribing clearly defined responsibilities in a discussion. This gives you greater control over what happens once students break into small groups for talk.

The quickest way to allocate roles is to ask students to label themselves A, B, C, and so on, and then outline a particular role for one or all of the students. This may be as simple as your saying, "Person B, you are going to instigate the discussion by sharing your ideas first," or, "Person A, it is your job to ask for evidence. How can you encourage your partner to support what they are saying by using the text?" By setting up the discussion in this way, you are making clear to your students what role you want them to play in moving their own and their classmates' thinking forward.

A number of different roles you could allocate to your students during talk tasks are outlined in Box 5.2.

BOX 5.2

ORACY IN ACTION: ROLES IN TRIOS

Trios are a particularly good grouping to use when allocating roles, as one student can be given a clearly defined job that helps strengthen the group's discussion or puts a spotlight on a specific skill. Below are some favorites.

SILENT SUMMARIZER

Student A and Student B have a discussion about a given topic or question. You may want to provide sentence stems to scaffold their conversation, as shown in figure 5.2. Meanwhile, Student C, the "silent summarizer," must remain silent while the discussion runs its course. They must then summarize the main points they have heard back to the other two group members. This highlights the importance of, and skill involved in, close listening. It also gives your students an opportunity to practice the cognitive skill of summarizing.

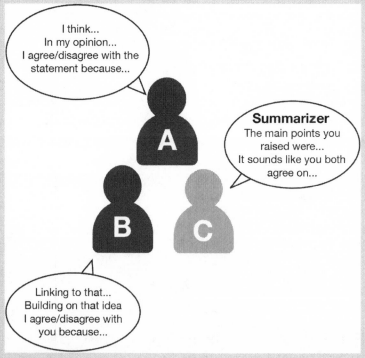

FIGURE 5.2
Silent Summarizer

This task works well for both louder, more dominant students, who have to remain silent and listen until others have finished speaking, and for quieter students, who have a chance to listen before they speak and have a clear role to fulfill when speaking.

TRIO QUESTIONER

This role is similar to the silent summarizer, except Student C is only allowed to ask questions. This could be centered around a topic or question, or a specific stimulus like a painting in art, a poem in English, or a table of results from an experiment in science. Again, sentence stems and question openers/prompts can be used, as shown in figure 5.3.

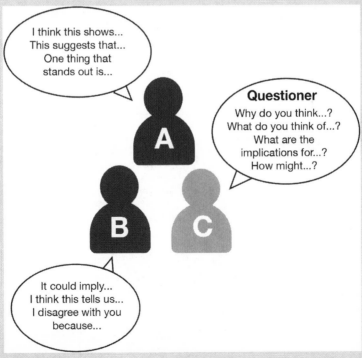

FIGURE 5.3
Trio Questionner

ORACY EXPERT

Student A and B have a discussion, while Student C, the "oracy expert," observes and then gives feedback on a specific aspect of the pair's oracy. For instance, the expert could give feedback on how well the pair listened to each other, or whether they gave reasons for their opinions.

PROTOCOLS

Protocols are rules that govern fair and equitable turn-taking. They provide a clear system for students to work out whose turn it is to speak, meaning group discussions can run independently of a teacher. Pairs won't need to use a protocol, as turn-taking in a pair merely requires the speakers to alternate, but for larger groupings protocols are a valuable tool to structure talk.

It may take some time to establish them with your students, but once using protocols becomes habit, you will reap the rewards: student-led, self-governing talk that runs smoothly.

You can create your own protocols—for example, teachers of younger students may be familiar with a "talking teddy," the holder of which is the only person allowed to speak. Here are three more protocols to get you started.

Pass and Go

Students are seated in a circle. One student starts by sharing their idea, and then passes to the next student to speak. Students take turns going around the circle, sharing their idea and then passing to the next person.

Pass and go works well in situations where you want a large number of ideas generated, and for everyone to have had a chance to speak. However, as it is follows a set pattern of moving talk around the circle, it makes it difficult for students to engage in the back-and-forth of discussion. It is most suited to collecting lots of ideas or ensuring everyone gets to make an opening or closing remark—for example, asking for everyone's first thoughts to kick off a discussion.

Thumbs In

When a student has an idea to share, they put their thumb out in front of them. Once the first speaker has finished speaking, they choose whose turn it is to speak next (from the students who have their thumbs out). Once that person has finished speaking, they choose the next speaker and so forth.

Thumbs in means that no single person has control over the discussion. It also facilitates a more natural flow, letting talk bounce between speakers.

Chaired Discussion

Each group needs to agree upon a chairperson. The chairperson should make sure their group's discussion is productive, with relevant and fairly distributed contributions from all. The main way they can do this is by deciding who speaks and by asking questions. The chairperson should hold back from always giving their own opinions and instead encourage others to share theirs. Box 5.3 has some tips to help your students be excellent chairs.

As your students become more confident and skillful at chairing, they can be introduced to further layers of nuance and greater responsibilities. For

---

BOX 5.3

ORACY IN ACTION: TOP TIPS FOR
BEING A CHAIR

1. Make sure you give everyone a chance to speak.

2. If you notice someone hasn't contributed, invite them in by saying their name or asking them a question.

3. If you think your group has reached an agreement, or if the discussion is becoming repetitive, summarize the main points so far to help the discussion move forward.

4. Be prepared to ask probing or clarifying questions, and encourage others to do so, too.

5. Being chair is a big responsibility. Make sure that everyone gets a chance to take on this role at some point.

instance, can they summarize what has been said thematically or ask probing questions to move the discussion forward?

Groupings, roles, and protocols organize classroom talk and, in doing so, help to keep talk learning focused and educationally productive. By being clear and precise about what form you want oracy tasks to take, the roles you want students to fulfill, and the protocols that need to be followed to ensure equity of contributions, you can retain a level of structure over student talk while also allowing students space to think freely for themselves.

QUESTIONS TO CONSIDER

- Which groupings work best in your classroom?
- How can you use roles to highlight specific skills you want your students to develop?
- How can you set up discussions so that your students are able to run them independently?

Elevate the Quality of Talk

It's all well and good for students to *know* what makes great talk, but that doesn't necessarily mean that they are able to do it. Talk scaffolds therefore give students the tools they need to reach a standard of talk they may not otherwise have achieved on their own.

It is easy to fall into the trap of thinking that because you have created opportunities for students to *use* oracy that you are *teaching* them oracy. Of course, practice is one part of learning. But for these opportunities to be as useful and as meaningful as possible, talk tasks should be scaffolded, enabling students to engage in a standard of talk they would not have been able to otherwise.

Scaffolding is a "process that enables a child or novice to solve a problem, carry out a task, or achieve a goal that would be beyond his unassisted efforts."[1] A scaffold acts as a temporary supportive structure for a student to complete a task they otherwise could not have.[2] As students become more confident, scaffolds will be needed less and less, until eventually they are not needed at all.

Let's consider this in relation to writing. To support students to produce the best possible written work, a teacher of writing might start by reading or deconstructing some examples, identifying the text's purpose, and using this to co-construct success criteria. The teacher might model writing an example on the board, provide a template or skeleton structure, and perhaps also supply individual sentence openers or key words. The teacher's high expectations for writing are met with a high level of scaffolding and support until the students have mastered the skills needed to write with proficiency.

To support your students to become excellent speakers, a similar level of scaffolding is required for oracy activities. This chapter provides some techniques to scaffold talk to help your students become confident and articulate speakers.

USE SENTENCE STEMS

Sentence stems (or sentence openers) are the simplest and most effective technique for scaffolding talk. At their most basic, they are phrases like "I agree because . . ." and "I disagree because . . . " As students become more adept talkers, the sentence stems you provide them with should become increasingly varied and sophisticated. Sentence stems can be used for pretty much everything!

The power of sentence stems comes from their ability to shape thinking as well as speaking. As Mercer and Littleton remind us, "Ways of thinking are embedded in ways of using language."[3] If you are prompted to start a sentence with "I agree/disagree because . . ." you are required to take a stance and justify your position. Sentence stems prompt students to think in a particular way and, as a result, are a useful scaffold for exploratory talk.

Start by considering the type of talk you want your students to engage in for a given talk task:

- What do you want this conversation, discussion, debate, or series of questions to sound like?
- What do you want your students to be thinking, and therefore what kinds of things should they be saying?
- How can your students sound like expert scientists, historians, mathematicians, art critics, and so on?

Use these ideas to create the sentence stems you think your students will need. Table 6.1 has some example sentence stems that are useful to scaffold exploratory talk. However, it is often preferable to create your own sentence stems for the task you have in mind. An example of this is discussed in Box 6.1.

BOX 6.1

TAILORING SENTENCE STEMS
TO SPECIFIC NEEDS

I was teaching a group of older students who were very comfortable saying "I agree/disagree because . . ." during group discussions. However, I felt that this response didn't do justice to the length or complexity of the point their peer had just made. In a sense, it let them off the hook, when really they needed to pinpoint their agreement or disagreement with their peer and explore it further.

The group needed sentence stems that prompted them to either identify the speaker or idea they were directly responding to. Without this, their discussion would never really get to the nitty-gritty of individual arguments, as their responses tended to remain broad-brush and general. I introduced sentence stems such as:

- I have a similar opinion to X because . . .
- X said that . . . which I agree/disagree with because . . .
- I recognize that . . . However, . . .
- I would like to challenge the idea that . . . because . . .

By using sentence stems that clearly named the person or idea they were responding to, the students were better able to home in on particular points of contention or agreement. This meant that their discussions moved more quickly into negotiating ideas, providing reasons for opinions, and developing deeper lines of inquiry around a single topic or theme.

—Alice Stott

Table 6.1. Sentence Stems Bank

To predict	I predict that . . .
	I think this will be about . . .
	I think the effect will be . . .
To compare and contrast	On the one hand . . . On the other hand . . .
	Another difference is that . . . Whereas . . .
	In contrast . . .
	Similarly, I think . . .
To evaluate	Overall, I think . . .
	In my opinion . . .
	On the one hand . . . But on the other hand . . .
	On balance, I think . . .
To explain	This is because . . .
	It is evident that . . . because . . .
	It is clear that . . . because . . .
	The reason for this is . . .
To sequence	First, . . .
	To begin with, . . .
	Second, . . .
	Then, . . .
	After, . . .
	Finally, . . .

When you are introducing your chosen sentence stems to students, display them on a board while they have their discussion and/or model using them before it is the students' turn to talk.

This isn't to say that by providing students with a sentence stem like "To build on what X said, I think . . ." they will automatically begin offering contributions that build on others' ideas. Your students may need to be taught what it means to build, challenge, predict, infer, or whichever other skill you want to highlight through your choice of sentence stem. However, by giving students the language to articulate those thought processes, you are helping them take the first step to thinking in that manner.

Moreover, sentence stems enable students to focus more on *what* it is they want to say than *how* to say it. Instead of thinking about the appropriate way to start their contribution to a discussion, students are freed up to think about the idea they want to share. This can be particularly helpful for quieter students, who may feel anxious about what to say when they go to speak, but have an idea they want to contribute.

Table 6.2. Sentence Stems to Agree/Disagree

I agree because . . .	*I disagree because . . .*
<ul><li>I agree and would like to add . . .</li><li>I have a similar opinion to . . . because . . .</li><li>I'd like to support that point because . . .</li><li>It may not seem like it, but X and I both agree about . . . because . . .</li><li>I am inclined to agree with the point that . . .</li><li>I wholeheartedly agree because . . .</li><li>I am absolutely convinced that . . . because . . .</li></ul>	<ul><li>I have a very different opinion than X because . . .</li><li>While . . . is an important consideration, it isn't as important as . . .</li><li>I don't see eye to eye with . . . because . . .</li><li>I agree with the outcome you want, but . . .</li><li>I am fundamentally opposed to this because . . .</li></ul>

Finally, sentence stems develop students' linguistic skills. They are a chance for students to rehearse certain words and phrases. Once they have grasped them, you can keep adding more variations that grow in sophistication and subtlety. For instance, consider some of the many possible ways in which and degrees to which students can agree or disagree shown in table 6.2.

Focusing on phrasing, through the use of sentence stems, grows the pool of language students can draw on and can support them to move between different degrees of formality. Sentence stems can also serve as a useful precursor to academic writing.

When students are first introduced to sentence stems, they can sound robotic or unnatural. It is true that they may seem clunky, especially at first, but then so are most techniques or skills when we first learn them. Yet with time, your students will start to use them with a naturalness and surety.

Once your students have grasped one set, mix things up and introduce another. As students become more confident using a range of sentence stems, the scaffold can fall away and students can start to make their own choices about how to open their sentences, introducing their own modifications and inventions.

MODEL WHAT YOU WANT

Children need to know what "good" talk or listening involves—and the easiest way to do this is to show them. Just as with great writing, where we point to classic texts or particularly effective passages, it can be powerful to hold up examples of great speakers or listeners. However, your examples don't need to come only from great speeches and momentous occasions, but also from everyday discussions and interactions.

Look to Stellar Examples

Find great examples of the talk you want your students to be doing, talk that follows similar conventions and uses similar skills. Do you want your students to speak as an expert with authority on an issue, chair a discussion, comment on an event, or give an elevator pitch? Where can you find examples of this type of talk being done well?

Once you have found a couple of examples, work out what exactly makes the speaker so good (and how they could do even better). Identifying skills from the Oracy Framework can help with this.

For instance, if you want your students to speak with authority when presenting their results from a scientific experiment, you may want to unpack an example from TV, such as a BBC special with Professor Brian Cox or the latest NASA press conference announcing a major breakthrough. What makes these good examples of this type of talk? Is it the choice of language and technical terminology (linguistic strand), or the speaker's detailed explanation (cognitive), or the speaker's ability to simplify complex ideas for a less knowledgeable audience (social and emotional)?

It can be just as useful for students to draw upon examples from real life. For example, you could ask your students to observe and report back on how the head teacher or principal speaks with authority in an assembly. By giving students a model for what "speaking with authority" looks like, and supporting them to identify the specific characteristics associated with talk in this context, you are better preparing them to speak in this style.

Create Your Own Examples

If anything, drawing on examples that are relatable, close to home, and current can be all the more powerful and useful. This can mean you, another adult, or your students being models for oracy. You could stage a conversation or discussion with another teacher or student, perform a poem by heart, or deliver a speech, as described in Box 6.2.

The advantage of doing this is that you can make sure whatever it is you want to draw attention to comes through. Want someone to model asking

BOX 6.2

MODELING ORACY FOR MY STUDENTS

When teaching my class of eight-year-olds about speech-making, I spent a lot of time unpacking famous examples with them to work out why they were so successful. However, I felt I needed a speech that contained all of the rhetorical devices I was planning on teaching—and so decided to write and perform a speech of my own.

When writing my speech, I made sure to include all of the features of speech-making that my students were going to learn about, such as rhetorical questions, the rule of three, metaphors, and similes. This gave my students a frame of reference for what they were aiming to achieve in their speeches, which we could deconstruct in class.

The process of writing and performing my own speech helped me to better understand what I was asking my students to do. It also meant that when some students felt nervous about memorizing and performing their speeches, I was able to relate!

—*Amy Gaunt*

really precise clarifying questions, listening attentively, or using tone of voice to add emphasis? Then you can be sure to show this in your example.

Your students can also act as models for the rest of the class. This can be particularly useful for showcasing great oracy in a discussion: gather the class around a successful group fishbowl style, or record a group to be watched back later and analyzed. Tasks like this not only strengthen students' understanding of "what good looks like," but also build their meta-language to talk about talk and to reflect on their own and others' talk.

It is also worth remembering that when it comes to modeling oracy, you don't always need to provide the perfect example. As much as it is useful to ask, "What makes this speaker or group good?" it is just as useful to ask,

"What could they be doing better?" If you, as the teacher, are modeling something and asking your students "What could I have done better?" you are modeling how to reflect on talk and use feedback to improve.

You Are a Model at All Times

Everything that you do and say within your classroom serves as a model for the students you teach. There are so many opportunities for you to model different oracy skills within your day-to-day practice, whether these are explicit and deliberate or incidental.

Using the same language you want students to be using, in your own talk and questioning, enables you to model its use in context. Similarly, if you want students to be building on, challenging, and summarizing each other's thinking in their discussions, you can mirror this in whole-class discussions.

You can also model individual skills, like inviting someone into a discussion or asking clarifying questions. Flag to students your metacognitive thought process as you are doing so: "I've noticed Sean hasn't spoken yet, and I'm going to invite him in now. What do you think, Sean?" or "Hang on, I'm not sure I understand. Can I just clarify, did you mean . . . ?"

Just as important as modeling the linguistic and cognitive aspects of oracy are the physical and social and emotional strands. Modeling the physical aspects of talk alongside the linguistic—using call-and-repeat to get students comfortable with specific words and phrases while using the intonation or gestures to best accompany them—reinforces meaning.

You can also model use of gestures, tone of voice, and facial expressions in your day-to-day demeanor. It is from watching you speak in an expressive manner that students are likely to pick up these same skills. Similarly, model what you want from listening by asking meaningful questions about, paraphrasing, or summarizing what has been said.

SCAFFOLD KEY WORDS AND PHRASES

Your students may need subject-specific, technical terminology or certain phrases to support them to talk confidently and with precision about a theme or topic.

The "which one does not belong" activity outlined in chapter 4 provides an excellent example as to how key words can be scaffolded. For instance, if presenting students with a set of 3D and 2D shapes, you may want to provide key mathematical vocabulary: *corner, symmetry, face, vertices, two-dimensional, three-dimensional,* etc. Alternatively, at the start of the activity you could invite students to suggest the key words they think they might need and collate a list on the board for them to use.

Providing students with a word or phrase bank to call upon when speaking gives them a chance to try out new language and hear it in their own and others' speech. This is a crucial mechanism through which we learn new language. The next chapter explores this relationship between speaking and vocabulary development in more detail.

QUESTIONS TO CONSIDER

- What would be the most useful sentence stems for your students? How might these vary according to subject, theme, or topic?
- How do you model oracy in your classroom?
- What do you need to equip your students with to support them to meet your high expectations for oracy?

NOTES

1. D. Wood, J. S. Bruner, and G. Ross, "The Role of Tutoring in Problem-Solving," *Journal of Child Psychology and Psychiatry* 17 (1976): 89–100.

2. M. F. Graves, S. Watts, and B. B. Graves, *Essentials of Classroom Teaching: Elementary Reading* (Boston: Allyn and Bacon, 1994), 44.

3. N. Mercer and K. Littleton, *Dialogue and the Development of Children's Thinking: A Sociocultural Approach* (London: Routledge, 2007), 26.

7

Cultivate Vocabulary

One specific aspect of talk that benefits greatly from careful and deliberate teaching is the use of language, namely vocabulary. For many children, their exposure to language and interaction through talk in the early years is vastly unequal. Consider the following findings:

- By the age of five, 75 percent of British children who experienced poverty persistently throughout the early years are below average in language development, compared to 35 percent who never experienced poverty.[1]
- In the UK, low-income children lag behind their middle-income counterparts at school entry by nearly one year in vocabulary, and by smaller but still substantial amounts in other types of cognitive development.[2]
- In the USA, children from low-income backgrounds have heard on average thirty million fewer words than their wealthier peers by the age of three.[3]

As teachers we must create classrooms that are language rich and encourage children to interact with a wide-ranging, diverse, and complex spread of vocabulary, through both speaking and listening.

For students who arrive at school already behind their peers in terms of language development, school is their second chance to acquire the rich and varied vocabulary they will need for success both in life and academically. However, this second chance comes with little certainty. "The Matthew Effect," named after a verse in the New Testament (Matthew 25:29), describes the phenomenon whereby the rich get richer while the poor get poorer. This effect has been widely argued to hold in several areas of education, such as reading, where success begets success. It has also been documented in vocabulary knowledge, where there is, as Law et al. argue, "a clear 'social gradient' for language, with children from the most disadvantaged groups having lower language skills than those in the least disadvantaged groups. . . . If we look at the longer-term impact of language delay, all studies appear to tell the same story—namely, that those from the most disadvantaged backgrounds are the least likely to catch up."[4] In this context, every opportunity for robust, rich vocabulary teaching needs to be grasped with both hands.

Oracy supports vocabulary acquisition in a number of ways. Classrooms filled with talk mean students have opportunities to hear new words in context; this provides an *input* of new language. In classrooms where opportunities for students to talk are plentiful, students also have occasion to use this vocabulary in their speech, and through this *output* take ownership of new language. Let's look at each function in turn.

INPUT: LISTENING

The first way that a child learns language is not out of a dictionary, glossary, or set text, but rather from the mouths of others: in speech, in context. Yet it tends to be the case that as children get older, the words they hear in speech are ones that they already know, and so "the source of later vocabulary learning shifts to written contexts—what children read."[5]

As Beck et al. note, this doesn't necessarily make sense: "The problem is that it is not so easy to learn word meanings from written context. Written context lacks many of the features of oral language that support learning new word meanings, such as intonation, body language, and shared physical surroundings. As such, written language is a far less effective vehicle for learning new words than oral language."[6]

The often-cited image that "reading and writing float on a sea of talk"[7] brings to mind this relationship clearly. In order to read or write using new vocabulary, children need to have heard and spoken the language themselves. So why accept that the tide of talk should recede as children become older and more familiar with language? It is through hearing new language and using it in speech that children will be able to read it, write it, and use it with fluency.

The assumption that once children have reached a basic proficiency in spoken language, they need to engage with written texts to learn new vocabulary, is false. There is no ceiling on the language that can be learned by listening, as seen in Box 7.1. A talk-rich classroom, where children and teachers model sophisticated and specialist language for each other, providing contextual clues and explanations of word meanings where necessary, builds vocabulary knowledge far more effectively than a dense text and accompanying glossary.

BOX 7.1

LISTENING TO CHALLENGING TEXTS IN CONTEXT

The idea that as children get older, the richness of spoken language they can encounter diminishes isn't borne out in reality. If anything, we do children a disservice if we don't give them opportunities to *listen* to challenging texts, just as we would want them to *read* challenging texts.

This was made startlingly clear to me when I took a group of students (ages eight to eleven) to listen to the mayor of London's Question Time. As school trips go, it was a bit of a gamble—not your usual day out at a theme park or on the beach! The plan was to give the students a real, weighty experience of oracy in a specific context: inside the corridors of power at City Hall.

However, as I tried to quietly settle a group of thirty excited schoolchildren into the chamber, where the mayor of London was already taking questions from assembly members, it occurred to me that the trip could well turn out to be a terrible mistake. Although I had done some teaching about the type of issues the mayor of London is responsible for, I felt like much of what was being talked about was likely to be impenetrable to the students: changes to subsidies on public transport, proposals to cut funding for the fire brigade, and measures to tackle rogue landlords. I waited nervously, looking out for any signs of the onset of fidgeting and whispering from the students. Instead, I was impressed by how attentively they listened and tried to follow the back-and-forth of the mayor's discussion.

On leaving the chamber, we stopped as a group to debrief and have lunch. The conversation ended up having the air of a post-match analysis, dissecting how the mayor had come back to each question, tried to mask anything he couldn't answer, and played the room. I was taken aback by how much the students had taken from what had been said. The contextual clues offered by City Hall, the students' expectations of the situation, and their predictions for what different people might say all fed into their overall understanding. This was layered with their reading of body language and tone of voice, which had supported them to work out where disagreements had arisen over particular issues.

While they may not have understood every word, it was clear that they did digest much of what had been said. Moreover, when talking about what they had seen, it was noticeable that students were using new phrases such as "public services" and deploying familiar language in new ways, such as describing "cuts" in spending.

This experience highlighted to me the value to be gained from letting children listen, to learn new things about the world and to learn new vocabulary. Had I given the minutes of a mayor's Question Time meeting to the same group of children, I have no doubt they would have struggled to access it, let alone be interested! Instead, the spoken context gave them the "clues" needed to make sense of what was being said and learn new language in context.

—*Alice Stott*

Table 7.1. **Supporting Vocabulary Development through Oracy**

Strand	Approach to Teaching New Vocabulary
Physical	How can you use your tone of voice, intonation and emphasis, gestures, facial expressions, and movement to give meaning to what you are saying?
Linguistic	How can you provide synonyms, antonyms, and alternative definitions in student-friendly language?
	How can you model new, challenging vocabulary in context?
Cognitive	How can you give relevant examples and make associations to other language, experiences, and concepts your students will already know?
	How can you support comprehension and inference, in the same way that you would for a written text (e.g., using pictures)?
Social and Emotional	How can you adapt what you say so that it is appropriate for your audience (e.g., for younger students) and find shared points of reference?

As a teacher, you can use the four strands of the Oracy Framework to support your students to make meaning from the complex language used in your classroom. Consider how you can use your own oracy skills to introduce new vocabulary, as suggested in table 7.1.

OUTPUT: SPEAKING

Rather than expecting students to leap from understanding a word's meaning straight into using new language in written work, oracy creates a space for students to try out, revise, and demonstrate their understanding of words.

By using newly learned vocabulary, students are able to take hold of its meaning and assimilate it into their lexicon. According to Beck et al., "Learning words well enough to express them is an important learning goal, and having words in one's productive vocabulary is generally viewed as a good measure of word ownership."[8] Getting students to speak, to use new vocabulary, and to hear themselves say words out loud is a key step toward truly learning a word.

Sentence Stems

The power of sentence stems to frame thinking and as a scaffold for language has already been discussed. However, it is worth highlighting that sentence stems are also a strategy for reinforcing specific target vocabulary, prompting students to use new language in their speech. Consider the following examples:

- I thought it was *inevitable* that . . .
- I felt *foreboding* when . . .
- The most *egotistical* character is . . . because . . .
- I agree/disagree that the play is a *tragedy* because . . .
- As an *environmentalist*, I would . . .

Each sentence stem draws the new language into the opener, ensuring that students use it; how they choose to end the sentence provides a good insight into how well they have understood the word's meaning.

Talking Points

Again, by implanting new vocabulary in a talking point,[9] students will need to grapple with the meaning of the word. Consider the following examples:

- Hamlet's death was *inevitable.*
- A parent-child relationship is an example of a *symbiotic* relationship.
- All 3D shapes have *vertices.*

Photo Fit

This is a playful way for students to engage with the meaning of a new word. Having introduced the word and its meaning to students, provide students with four to six images that each depict the word's meaning in a different context. For instance, for the word *relieved* the images might show a key in a door, a parent meeting a child, someone making a cake, and a student receiving high marks on an assignment.

Working in pairs or trios, students should lay the set of images in front of them. Ask each student to try to form a sentence that uses the word accurately. They pick up the relevant image and tell their sentence to their group: for example, "Susan was relieved to find that she had not burned the cake," or "I was relieved when I realized I hadn't left my key in the door." If a student's sentence doesn't quite make sense, model how to reformulate the sentence and encourage other students in the group to do this.

The task could be made competitive, with students collecting the images for the sentences they have mastered (this would work better with six or more images).

Alternatively, you could set up the task as an exercise in storytelling: rather than each student forming a sentence independently of what has been said previously, each speaker needs to link what they are saying to what has been said before and, in doing so, create a story that includes all the pictures (and uses the target vocabulary many times over!).

Summary Bullseye

A summary bullseye helps to consolidate vocabulary that has already been taught to students. It requires you to have identified about fifteen words, of varying levels of difficulty or familiarity to your students, that are key to their summary of a topic, text, or process. They should all be words that students have been taught before; they could be academic or technical, alongside some more common and familiar language.

You then need to organize these words into a "bullseye": the easiest, worth one point, in the outer circle; the next hardest, worth three points, in the middle circle; the hardest words, worth five points, in the inner circle.

Below are two examples. The first example, Figure 7.1, has been created to follow reading the first few chapters of *The Curious Incident of the Dog in the Night-Time* by Mark Haddon.[10]

The second example, shown in Figures 7.2 and 7.3, comes from a science classroom where students have been learning about the water cycle. It provides the technical language needed to successfully describe the water cycle.

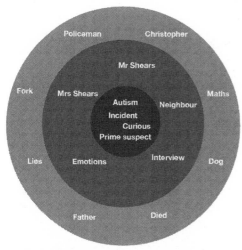

FIGURE 7.1
The Curious Incident Summary Bullseye

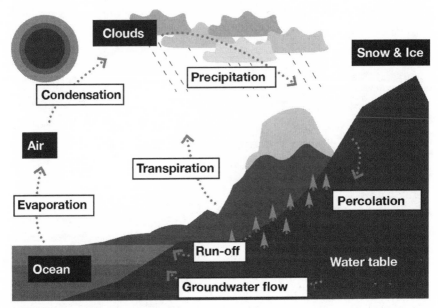

FIGURE 7.2
The Water Cycle

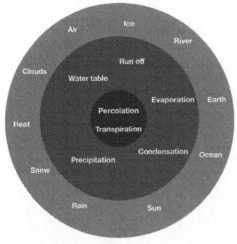

	Tally	Total
5 point words		
3 point words		
1 point words		
Overall total		

FIGURE 7.3
The Water Cycle Summary Bullseye

Working in pairs, students take turns summarizing what they have been learning: in the first example, providing a summary explanation of the plot of the book so far, and in the second, providing a summary of the water cycle.

Before embarking on this task, it is worth spending time as a class defining what constitutes a good summary:

- It covers the main points without merely becoming a list.
- It is logically sequenced, for instance by using time connectives (it doesn't jump around).
- It is concise (rather than repetitive).

Students can have their summary bullseye sheet in front of them (after all, the purpose is for it to act as a prompt for them to use new vocabulary as they speak), and should be encouraged to spend some time thinking about how they are going to include the words on the sheet before they start.

The speaker's aim is to accurately use as much of the target language as possible in their summary. Their partner listens to them doing this, and ticks off the words as they use them (there are no additional points for using the same word multiple times!) to give a total score at the end. The students then swap roles, so that they each get a score at the end of the task.

Depending on the level of cunning among your students, you may need to institute a time limit (to mitigate against the student who just goes on and on until they have got every word ticked off, at the expense of what they are saying having made sense). The points system can also lead to some students shoe-horning in vocabulary, but not necessarily using it correctly. The listener needs to know that they can challenge anything they think is inaccurate use of vocabulary before awarding points for it!

This task turns using new language into a game—and the competition can help to motivate! Not only does it motivate students to use words they may not have otherwise used, but it also incentivizes their partner to listen closely for the point-worthy words and for any potentially inaccurate uses, which can be picked up on and checked at the end.

The summary bullseye raises students' awareness of the "value" of different words and in doing so prompts them to expand their vocabulary. It is also a useful tool for maintaining new vocabulary, as you (and your students) can keep returning to it and adding new words as you go.

Discussions about Words

Vocabulary itself can be a stimulus for discussion. Pose questions about language such as:

- Is X the opposite of Y?
- What is the opposite of X?
- Can you be both X and Y?
- Would you rather be X or Y?
- Who is the best example of someone who is X, and why?

These types of questions encourage students to develop their understanding of words. They also create a space for students to air any misconceptions, which you can then address.

Use the Physical Strand to Explore Word Meanings

Being playful with the physical aspects of oracy also lets you and your students explore words and become confident using them. This could be as simple as saying new vocabulary aloud together: "Say the words with me" or "My turn, your turn," while changing your tone of voice, slowing down the sounds, or placing the emphasis in funny places.

Alternatively, you could use gestures and facial expressions to act out word meanings: How would you look if you were feeling X or Y? What would you be doing if you were X or Y?

Having a wide and varied vocabulary, and being able to deploy this language with deliberateness and precision, is fundamental to being a great speaker. However, it is through speaking and listening that we develop a wide and varied vocabulary. In this way, teaching vocabulary *through* oracy and *for* good oracy are mutually reinforcing.

QUESTIONS TO CONSIDER

- How do you model new and challenging vocabulary in your speech and provide your students with clues to support their understanding?
- How can you encourage your students to use specific words or phrases you would like them to use in speech?

NOTES

1. Communication Trust, *Talking about a Generation: Current Policy, Evidence and Practice for Speech, Language and Communication* (London: Communication Trust, 2017), http://www.thecommunicationtrust.org.uk/media/540327/tct_talkingaboutageneration_report_online.pdf.

2. J. Waldfogel and E. Washbrook, *Low Income and Early Cognitive Development in the UK* (London: Sutton Trust, 2010).

3. B. Hart and T. R. Risley, "The Early Catastrophe: The 30 Million Word Gap by Age 3," *American Educator*, Spring 2003, https://www.aft.org/sites/default/files/periodicals/TheEarlyCatastrophe.pdf.

4. J. Law et al., cited in Communication Trust, *Talking about a Generation*.

5. I. L. Beck, M. G. McKeown, and L. Kucan, *Bringing Words to Life: Robust Vocabulary Instruction*, 2nd ed. (New York: Guildford Press, 2013), 5.

6. Ibid.

7. J. Britton, "Writing and the Story of the World," in B. Kroll and C. Wells, eds., *Explorations in the Development of Writing: Theory, Research, and Practice* (New York: Wiley, 1983), 3–30.

8. Beck, McKeown, and Kucan, *Bringing Words to Life*, 58.

9. L. Dawes, *Talking Points: Discussion Activities in the Primary Classroom* (Oxon: David Fulton, 2012).

10. M. Haddon, *The Curious Incident of the Dog in the Night-Time* (London: Vintage, 2003).

8

Teach Listening, Too

It has been said that listening is to speaking what reading is to writing. Listening enables students to engage critically with complex ideas, learn from their peers, and hear new vocabulary in context. To speak well, students must first learn to listen well. Of course, listening is also important in its own right and is crucial if we are to engage with and, more importantly, learn from the world around us. However, listening, just like speaking, is a skill that needs to be taught; students will not become great listeners without explicit instruction in how to do so.

LISTENING SKILLS

"They just won't listen!" is an oft-heard teacher refrain. However, are teachers really lamenting their students' lack of listening skills, or are they complaining that they struggle to stay quiet? Remaining silent while someone else is speaking is fundamental to good listening, but there are many more aspects of this important skill that are worth exploring with your students.

The Oracy Framework is a useful tool for identifying and categorizing listening skills. Consider the four strands of oracy (physical, cognitive, linguistic, and social and emotional) and which listening skills sit beneath each of them.

Physical

The physical markers of listening are often the easiest to teach and usually the best place to start, especially with younger students. Physical markers of listening include:

- Facing the speaker
- Making eye contact
- Remaining calm and still; not distracting others

Collectively, these skills are sometimes referred to as "full body listening" to encapsulate the idea that good listening is demonstrated through body language.

It is important to talk to students about these skills explicitly. Why not draw out the skills outlined above and create a checklist to be referred to before any group activity? With younger children, visual cues are helpful; you could prominently display and regularly refer to an annotated picture demonstrating "good listening." This could simply be a photo of a group of children engaging in group discussion, sitting, facing each other, and looking at the person who is speaking.

Finally, before starting any group discussion activity, ask students to assume a good listening position and begin the task only when everybody has done this. If students are sitting at tables and chairs, it is worth asking them to consider how they can alter their position to allow for better listening. For example, they may be better placed and less distracted if they move their chairs away from the table and into a circle.

Cognitive

Listening is a cognitive process through which we develop understanding. The way that a student responds to what has been said is therefore a good indicator of listening and understanding. Cognitive markers of listening include:

- Summarizing
- Asking questions
- Building on what has been said

These skills require students to respond in different ways. To summarize, students must engage critically with what has been said, identifying the main ideas. Similarly, to ask questions to clarify their understanding or to challenge a speaker, students must both actively monitor their own understanding and critically examine the speaker's ideas. Finally, to build on what someone has said, students must identify and share relevant ideas.

The cognitive skills of listening can be more difficult to teach than the physical ones, but are no less important. It is worth, for example, explicitly teaching students how to summarize a discussion. You may ask students to listen for key themes or ideas and then restate these in a given number of points. To build understanding of effective summary, it is a good idea to provide students with examples of summaries of varying quality and ask them to decide which is most effective. These could include examples of summaries that do not capture the main ideas or that are excessively detailed.

Asking questions, whether to clarify understanding or encourage a speaker to critically evaluate their ideas, is an important aspect of listening and a crucial skill to teach. It can be useful to teach students about different types of questions, when best to use these, and for what purpose. A good place to start is the difference between clarifying and probing questions, a more detailed explanation of which can be found in chapter 3.

Linguistic

The linguistic skill most closely linked to listening is paraphrasing. Listening to someone and rephrasing what they have said demonstrates that you have both listened to and understood what they are saying. What's more, paraphrasing can also be beneficial to a speaker, as hearing someone express what they have said using different words may help to clarify or elucidate their thinking.

When teaching students to paraphrase, first explore the difference between paraphrasing and summarizing. Paraphrasing is when you explain someone's ideas in your own words, whereas summarizing involves taking the main ideas and conveying these more simply and succinctly.

Once students have understood the difference between these two skills, take regular opportunities to model to students how to both summarize effectively and paraphrase accurately. For example, when a student answers a question or gives an opinion, ask someone else in the class to paraphrase or summarize what has been said.

After listening to a student paraphrase another's ideas, ensure that you praise them not just for the content of what was said, but for how well they conveyed their partner's ideas. For example, you might say, "Well done, that was excellent paraphrasing; you explained your partner's ideas using your own words." This reinforces both the student and their classmates' under-standing of this important skill.

Social and Emotional

We often talk about the effect a speaker can have on a listener, but we rarely talk about the reverse, how a listener affects a speaker. However, whether someone is listening and how they show this can have a profound impact on someone who is speaking. Consider the difference between talking to a person who looks bored and disinterested and speaking to someone who smiles and offers nods of encouragement or asks questions.

The social and emotional aspects of listening encompass this relation-ship between listener and speaker and relate, in particular, to how we make a speaker feel heard. The social and emotional markers of listening include:

- Smiling
- Nodding
- Offering words of encouragement
- Reacting and refocusing (for example, laughing when a speaker says some-thing amusing, but then refocusing on what they are saying)

A great game to teach the social and emotional aspects of listening is Back-to-Back, an explanation of which can be found in Box 8.1.

THE LISTENING LADDER

To help our students become better listeners, we must explicitly teach these skills; however, we must also provide students with opportunities to reflect on how well they listen. This could be as simple as, after a discussion, asking students to explain whether they were good listeners or not, giving reasons. In order to do this, students must understand what constitutes good listening, or not, and be able to describe this.

One way to encourage students to be reflective about listening is by using the Listening Ladder, detailed in figure 8.1. The Listening Ladder sets out the various listening skills explored in this chapter and orders them in terms of complexity. After a discussion or listening activity, students can decide which rung of the ladder they reached and set targets for where they will get to next

---

BOX 8.1

ORACY IN ACTION: BACK-TO-BACK

In this game two students stand back-to-back with each other. One is assigned the role of listener and the other, speaker. The listener asks the speaker a simple question, such as "What did you do over the weekend?" or "Who is your favorite sportsperson of all time and why?" which they answer. The person listening must ensure that the speaker knows they are listening by, for example, offering verbal reassurance and encouragement. This is made more difficult because the speaker cannot see the listener and the usual markers of listening, such as smiling or nodding, are therefore obsolete.

This game is a handy springboard for a discussion about the importance of the social and emotional aspects of listening. It can be useful to ask the speaker whether they felt they were listened to, how they knew this, and how this made them feel. It is then worth exploring with students why it is more difficult to be a good listener when you are back-to-back with someone. It is sometimes only when our ability to give eye contact, nod, smile, and so on is removed that we realize how important these cues are to show someone we are listening.

---

time. Students cannot climb to the next rung until they have achieved the skill outlined on the previous rung.

The Listening Ladder could also be used in a number of other ways. During small-group discussions, one student could remain silent and take responsibility for monitoring the group's listening and decide which rung on the ladder they got to. Alternatively, it could be used as a whole-class collective reward system for listening during whole-class discussions. When you are confident the majority of the class has climbed to the next rung, you can color the previous one in and use this as a barometer for the whole group's progress. When the whole ladder is colored in, the class can be rewarded for being top listeners!

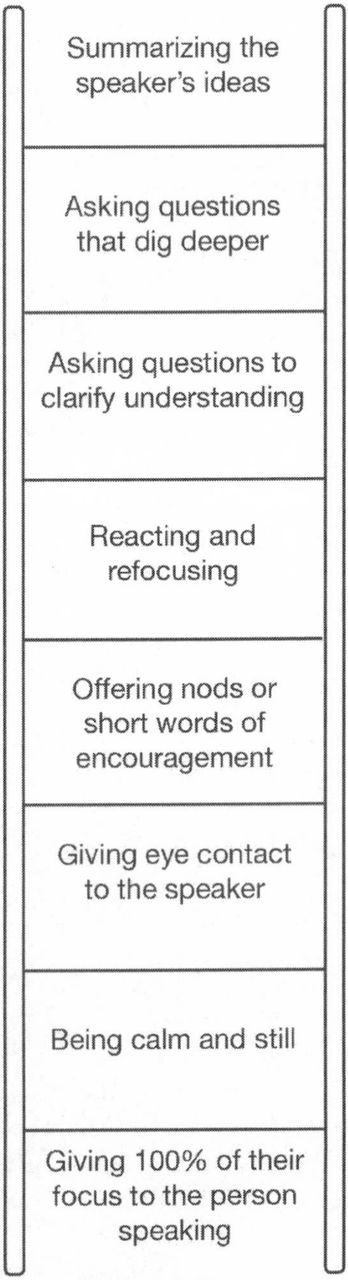

FIGURE 8.1
The Listening Ladder

Summarizing the
speaker's ideas

Asking questions
that dig deeper

Asking questions to
clarify understanding

Reacting and
refocusing

Offering nods or
short words of
encouragement

Giving eye contact
to the speaker

Being calm and still

Giving 100% of their
focus to the person
speaking

MACRO LISTENING AND MICRO LISTENING

Another interesting way that has been used to conceptualize listening is through the distinction between macro listening and micro listening. Once students have mastered the fundamental tenets of listening described in this chapter, it can be interesting to explore these with students. Put simply, macro listening is listening out for the bigger picture. What emotions is the speaker feeling? What is the subtext to what they are saying? In contrast, micro listening involves paying attention to, and remembering, the finer detail of what is being said. Table 8.1 outlines the difference between these two types of listening.

Table 8.1.

Micro Listening	Macro Listening
• What points did the speaker raise? • What facts, details, or dates did the speaker share? • How did the speaker start and end what they were saying?	• How is the speaker feeling? • What is the speaker not saying? • What do the speaker's tone of voice, body language, and facial expressions convey?

Both of these types of listening are useful in different contexts. When listening to a lecture or talk on something you care about, you may wish to micro listen so that you do not miss any information being shared. However, when listening to a friend describe a potential new job, macro listening may be more appropriate in order to gain a sense of how they're really feeling about this change. For example, are they feeling excited, overwhelmed, or unsure?

In reality, we all regularly employ both micro and macro listening, sometimes simultaneously. However, the distinction can be a useful one to make to students to help them become more aware of the complexity of listening.

Once you have introduced students to this concept, put their skills into practice with the activities outlined in Box 8.2.

Listening is a skill that is often taken for granted. However, it is the foundation upon which all oracy sits. Investing time developing this important skill will help your students become accomplished listeners, and therefore speakers.

BOX 8.2

ORACY IN ACTION: DIFFERENT TYPES
OF LISTENING

MICRO VS. MACRO LISTENING

Split students into groups of four. Ask two of the students to have
a discussion; this could be about anything, but it works best if the
subject is something controversial or something they are both
passionate about. One of the other students is assigned the role
of micro listener and the other, macro listener. After the discussion both students can offer feedback to their group on what they
noticed. The micro listener should recall most of the points made
by the speakers, whereas the macro listener should have noticed
the speakers' feelings, perspective, or agenda.

BUZZ WORD

This game, which teaches micro listening, involves one student
telling a story to their classmates, who are listening for a key
word, such as *bananas*. Once they hear the word they have to
buzz in or raise their hand; the first person to do this is the win-
ner and gets to go next. The best players tease their audience by
saying similar words or words that begin with the same sound
such as, "Then I ate some b . . . eautiful pineapple." To be successful in this game, players must pay careful attention to what
is being said.

QUESTIONS TO CONSIDER

- Do you explicitly teach listening?
- How can you celebrate and praise listening?
- How can you encourage your students to be reflective about their listening?

9

Embrace Oracy for Your Quiet Students

There are many students for whom incorporating more opportunities for talk in the classroom will be an exciting, invigorating venture. They feel comfortable sharing their ideas with others and enjoy working as part of a group. However, there are other, quieter students who prefer to work independently and for whom group work can be a difficult and nerve-racking task.

Many teachers, quite understandably, worry that a focus on oracy in the classroom will amplify the voices of the loudest students in their classrooms at the expense of these quieter students. However, if we believe in the importance of talk in the classroom and the benefits this can bring, then it is vital that we find ways to support all students to participate in classroom dialogue.

Every child is different; there isn't one strategy to support someone to participate in classroom talk that will work for all your students. Each student struggling to find their voice in the classroom has different barriers preventing them from participating. Some students may have diagnosed speech, language, and communication needs or other special needs. It is important that teachers find ways to support these students to access classroom discussion, and there are many specialists who have already written extensively on this.

For this reason, this chapter will not focus on ways to support students with specific speech, language, and communication needs, but rather how to create a classroom in which every child, including the quiet child, feels that their voice is valued.

CLASSROOM CULTURE

The classroom should be a safe environment in which every student feels that what they have to say matters. The first step to achieving this is to create a class set of discussion guidelines or ground rules for talk, as outlined in chapter 3.

Discussion guidelines set the expectations for talk in the classroom and help create a classroom culture conducive to talk. Explicitly stating as part of these guidelines that students should invite others to contribute to a discussion sets a powerful precedent. The success of a group's discussion no longer relies simply on the quality of individual contributions, but rather how successfully the members are able to work together as a group. For quieter children, simply being asked their opinion may be enough to make them feel their voice is valued and encourage them to contribute.

A classroom culture in which talk flourishes can take time to create. For some children who fear giving an incorrect answer or getting something wrong, it may take a long time for them to realize that it is acceptable to share a partially formed or incorrect idea. It may take even longer for them to develop the resilience to have someone challenge that idea.

In these cases, it is important that the teacher models both making mistakes and sharing undeveloped ideas for others to build on. It may also be beneficial to avoid praising "correct answers," but instead noting a student's thought process, effort, or simply that they felt brave enough to share their idea with others.

SENTENCE STEMS

Many of the tools for building a talk-rich classroom set out in this book, although not specifically designed to support quiet children to contribute, will have a big impact on these students. For example, providing students with sentence stems to help them structure their ideas during a discussion or when answering a teacher's question is a good idea for all students, but is particularly important for reluctant speakers.

A sentence stem allows a child to concentrate on what they want to say instead of how to start their sentence. For a quiet student, just having a well-rehearsed sentence starter, a scaffold upon which to hang their ideas, can go some way to removing the anxiety they may feel when sharing these ideas with others.

ROLES

Another strategy that is beneficial for all pupils, but that is particularly beneficial for quiet students, is assigning students clear roles during talk, discussed further in chapter 5. For many quiet students, anxiety arises from being unclear about the expectations for talk in a given context. For example, if a student is simply asked to "talk about" or "discuss" something in a group, they may be unclear about how many or what sort of contributions they are expected to make.

Assigning quieter students roles such as "silent summarizer" or "questioner" means that this is not the case. The "silent summarizer" is particularly effective, as the quiet student does not take part in an initial discussion and instead summarizes the group's discussion at the end, having had time to listen and carefully consider their response.

GROUPINGS

The way students are grouped during a talk activity can have a big impact on a quiet student's willingness to contribute. Both the size and composition of a group are important factors worth considering when planning for classroom talk. A quiet student may feel more comfortable, for example, working in a smaller group in which there are fewer competing voices. Trios are particularly effective, as two students can talk while a third, more reluctant speaker can join in when they feel ready.

In larger groups, it is worth carefully considering the composition of the group. It is often tempting to create groups that mix louder, more dominant students with less confident or quieter students. From a teacher's perspective, this is reassuring, as discussion is likely to flow; however, this group may be dominated by the louder voices. Instead, consider grouping quieter, more reluctant speakers together. When removed from the need to compete with others for airtime, these students will often contribute more, sometimes surprising themselves with the volume of their contributions.

TALK TOKENS

An equitable culture of classroom talk, in which everybody's voice is both heard and valued, requires quiet students to speak up and louder and more dominant students to speak less and listen more. A great way to create a more equal balance of talk in your classroom is by introducing "talk tokens."

Talk tokens—which could be counters, beads, or pieces of dried pasta—visually represent contributions to a discussion. When a student contributes to a discussion, they "spend" their token by placing it in a central pot. Issuing each student with a set number of talk tokens encourages them to think carefully about each contribution they make, as once a student has run out of tokens they cannot add anything else to the discussion. Tokens cannot be borrowed or traded!

This ensures that there is a more even balance of talk during a discussion, as each student in a group can only make a set number of contributions. Students that usually dominate a discussion will quickly learn to think carefully about when they spend their tokens, meaning that there is more space in a discussion for reluctant contributors to share their thoughts. This strategy also provides quiet students with an incentive to join in, as their contributions are more easily monitored and can be tracked over time. What's more, the physical act of spending a token can be quite powerful.

In its simplest form, this strategy is most appropriate for younger students; however, it can be adapted for older students by making it more complex. For instance, you could distribute different colored counters to denote different types of contribution, such as challenges and clarifying or probing questions.

PERSONAL TARGETS

Of course, these strategies may not work for everyone and it is entirely possible that, after exhausting these ideas, one or two of your students will still be unwilling to actively participate in talk activities. For these students, you may need to take a more personalized approach: talk to them, and find out what their barriers are and how you can help them overcome these.

Sometimes it is helpful to observe these students in other settings. Are they still quiet on the playground or when their parents pick them up from school? If their reluctance to speak is reserved only for the classroom, how can you create the conditions for them to feel confident sharing their ideas?

For some students, it may be beneficial to share the topic of a discussion or the setup of a talk activity the day before it takes place. This means they have time to consider what they might say prior to a discussion and may mean they are more likely to contribute. For younger students, you could also create a personalized reward chart, awarding them a star each time they contribute to a class discussion. When they reach a given number of stars, they could be rewarded with a certificate, a phone call home, or a treat of their choice! A case study, outlining how personal targets helped a quiet child find her voice, is included in Box 9.1.

BOX 9.1

BUILDING A QUIET STUDENT'S CONFIDENCE

Last year, the eight- and nine-year-olds in my class were preparing to give a two-minute speech on something they were passionate about to an audience of parents and caregivers. Most students were really excited about this; however, there was one particularly quiet child who was not.

My colleague Anna worked with this student to ensure that she felt able to take part and so that she gained the satisfaction of doing something that she previously did not feel confident enough to do. Together they developed a set of personal targets, such as to volunteer to answer a teacher's question or to chair a group discussion, and then worked toward achieving these goals.

First, Anna created a questionnaire to identify which situations the student did and didn't feel confident speaking in. Next, she talked to the student about what would help her to feel more confident in these situations—sitting with a friend, for example.

Anna also read a number of books with her, such as *Willow's Whispers*,[1] a picture book about a child who struggles to be heard. This prompted a conversation around quietness that was centered on the character in the book rather than the student in question.

To prepare for the final event, the student practiced a number of times in front of both adults and fellow students whom she felt comfortable with. Watching her perform her speech at the final event and visibly grow in confidence as she got further into the speech was a proud moment for her teachers!

—*Amy Gaunt*

NOTE
1. L. Button, *Willow's Whispers* (New York: Kids Can Press, 2010).

Finally, it is easy to think that if child is not actively participating in a discussion that they are not gaining anything from it. However, it is important to remember that even if a student does not contribute to a discussion, they can still listen to and learn from the contributions of their peers. In fact, quieter students may gain more from a discussion than their more boisterous peers, as they are likely to be better listeners, concentrating on others' contributions rather than thinking about what they are going to say next.

Of course, if a quiet child does not contribute to a discussion, classmates will miss out on the undoubtedly valuable thoughts the student has, and the student will miss out on the joy of their ideas being heard. For these reasons, it is important to find ways to support quiet students to participate. It is crucial, however, that quiet students are never forced to contribute; this is likely to increase their anxiety around speaking and may make them less likely to contribute in the future. Instead, teachers should concentrate on creating an inclusive classroom, conducive to talk, in which all students are able to find their voice.

QUESTIONS TO CONSIDER

- How do you differentiate or scaffold talk-based activities so that quiet students feel able to contribute?
- Are your quiet students quiet all the time?
- How can you encourage more dominant students to speak less and listen more?

10

Talk about Talk

Talk is an important lever for learning. It is the means through which we draw out and develop student understanding of ideas or concepts and through which we provide them with feedback. However, though talk is frequently used to assess and develop understanding across the curriculum, it is rare that we reflect on talk as an end in itself.

To improve in any skill, students need the chance to reflect on and learn from their performance and reapply this learning in a new context. Oracy is no exception, and many of the most powerful learning experiences you create in your classroom will be driven by students giving and receiving feedback, as well as reflecting on their own talk. To do this, it is vital that you and your students have an understanding of what makes good talk and a shared language to describe it. In short, you should be talking about talk!

A SHARED LANGUAGE

The four strands of oracy outlined in the Oracy Framework and your discussion guidelines or ground rules for talk, detailed in chapter 3, provide an excellent basis for developing a shared language for oracy in the classroom. Simply having a set of guidelines outlining what constitutes good talk in a given situation enables you to give students feedback on an aspect of their oracy and, crucially, helps them understand how to improve.

Developing your own language to describe talk, specific to the needs of your students, can also be a powerful way to support students to reflect on and improve their oracy skills. A case study of this in practice is set out in Box 10.1.

DEVELOPING LANGUAGE TO SUIT THE NEEDS OF YOUR CLASS

As I started to integrate more talk into my lessons, I noticed that some potentially very productive discussions veered off track because of one student who, while sharing an idea vaguely linked to the topic at hand, sent the discussion off in completely the wrong direction.

To help students become aware of this and to avoid this pitfall in the future, I introduced the terms *derailer*, someone who derails the discussion by sending it off track, and *navigator*, someone who gets the discussion back on track. In order for students to become familiar with these terms, I created a simple fictional transcript of a discussion and asked students to identify the navigators and derailers.

After learning the language to describe this phenomenon, pupils were able to identify when this happened and take steps to avoid discussions veering off track in the future. In fact, the pupils in my class became so familiar with these terms that I would often hear them asking others in their group to kindly not derail their discussion.

A colleague of mine who noticed that pupils in her class were often obstinate, refusing to change their mind in a discussion, introduced the terms *rock* and *water* to her class. A *rock* in a discussion is someone who refuses to change their mind or consider someone else's perspective or proposed course of action. *Water* denotes that someone is more flexible and willing to change their ideas, changing their position over the course of the discussion. At the end of a discussion, students were asked to reflect on whether they had played the rock or the water and whether this was the appropriate choice and why.

—*Amy Gaunt*

One of the simplest ways to develop a shared language for oracy in the classroom is through praising students consistently and liberally for the oracy skills that you are trying to embed. This works well on two levels. First, it brings oracy skills to life as you praise students for embodying them. Secondly, as students value praise, this also motivates them to employ these skills. In this way, it is a self-reinforcing cycle; as students become more aware of these skills, they are more likely to employ them, which in turn earns them praise.

How you praise students for oracy will depend on what you are working with them on. A teacher of young children focusing on students giving reasons for their opinions may praise the correct use of the word *because* when a student is explaining their ideas, rather than praise the ideas themselves. A teacher of older students may praise a student for being concise and grouping ideas when summarizing the key points of a discussion, rather than praise the content of the summary itself.

When praising students' oracy it is easy to fall back on comments about their gestures or the volume of their voice, as these tend to be the most readily identifiable features of talk. To ensure you are praising all of the elements that make up good talk, plan for oracy-specific praise across the four strands, as exemplified in table 10.1.

Table 10.1

Physical	Linguistic	Cognitive	Social and Emotional
Amazing, you were speaking at just the right volume for a trio discussion! Your body language showed me that you were very open to other people's ideas.	Great use of specialist vocabulary; you sounded like an expert! I loved the image you created of . . . All of the words you chose reinforced a sense of . . . The way you spoke made you sound like an authority on this.	It really helped me to understand your thinking when you used *first, then, finally.* You offered a great challenge! The example you gave was particularly powerful because . . .	Well done for inviting someone into the discussion. I know you are listening really well because your body language and eye contact are showing me that. You spoke really passionately and confidently. Well done!

METACOGNITION

Using oracy-specific language to give students praise or feedback also raises student awareness of the metacognitive processes underpinning these skills. Talk is, for the most part, something we do unthinkingly and upon which we rarely reflect. Students must become conscious of the often unconscious processes underlying talk before analyzing and improving these practices.

Evans and Jones describe this process in three stages. First, there is the moment that a child becomes conscious of a strategy or skill employed in talk. This is termed *aware use*. When a child is able to choose the best strategy or deploy a skill appropriate to the task at hand, this is known as *strategic use*. The highest level of understanding is reached at *reflective use*, when children are able to evaluate the effectiveness of the choices they have made and set targets for future improvement.[1]

Let's consider how this would apply in practice using the example of turn-taking. A child may become aware of this socially important skill during an activity in which they are unable to contribute because other children have dominated the discussion. Choosing to use a strategy, such as a protocol to regulate turn-taking, rather than speaking over others, means a child is becoming strategic in their understanding of talk.

The final stage in a child's understanding comes when they are able to reflect on their choices—for instance, reflecting on their role in bringing another child into a discussion or whether the balance of talk in a conversation was appropriate.

To support reflective, metacognitive thinking in oracy it is useful to employ oracy-specific models for feedback and reflection. These can develop students' understanding of the unconscious processes underlying talk, as well as reinforce the shared language for oracy you are developing in the classroom.

TALK DETECTIVES

One particularly effective strategy is to hand responsibility for monitoring discussions over to a couple of students or "talk detectives" who have a set of talk-focused success criteria (these could be drawn from your class discussion guidelines). Equipped with a clipboard, the talk detectives sneak around the classroom eavesdropping on the discussions going on and noting the things they hear to offer feedback to the class. These observations, which should be framed positively, reinforce students' understanding of the components of effective discussion.

Two different examples of talk detectives' recording sheets can be found in figures 10.1 and 10.2. Box 10.2 describes how this strategy works in practice.

Mystery to solve:
What does good oracy look like?

	Person or group name
Invited someone else to contribute	
Challenged a group member	
Summarized a group member's ideas	
Clarified somebody in their group's ideas	
Built on somebody else's ideas	
Changed their mind	
Came to a shared agreement	

FIGURE 10.1
Talk Detectives (Discussion Guidelines)

Mystery to solve: What does good oracy look like?

	Strand	Person or group name
	Physical - Are they speaking loudly & clearly? - Are they using hand gestures?	
	Cognitive - Are they giving reasons for their opinions? - Are they asking questions?	
	Linguistic - Are they using ambitious vocabulary?	
	Social & Emotional - Are they tracking the speaker? - Are they making sure everyone gets a turn to speak?	

FIGURE 10.2
Talk Detectives (The Oracy Framework)

BOX 10.2

TALK DETECTIVES IN PRACTICE

Talk detectives have become invaluable to me during discussion-based lessons. Not only do they help students to reflect on their oracy skills, but they have also proved to be a highly effective behavior management tool. Lots of students in my class clamor to be given the role of talk detective, as they enjoy having the freedom to move between groups and the authority to offer feedback to the rest of the class at the end of the lesson. The addition of a clipboard, as a prop to make the role official and important, adds an extra layer of excitement and can help to hook disengaged students.

I emphasize that detectives must move between groups without disturbing anything that is going on, only noting down their evidence using the sheet that provides a clear focus for their feedback. As the detectives remain silent for the main part of the lesson, allocating this role to students who have a tendency to dominate or derail discussions can create time for other students to speak up.

—*Alice Stott*

FILMING DISCUSSIONS

Another way to raise students' awareness of talk is to film their discussions and watch them as a class. This supports students to analyze what makes good talk and to evaluate the choices made by themselves or their peers.

Reflection of this kind can be structured in two ways. It could be set up as a very open-ended task where students watch the clip without prompts and are encouraged to discuss how effective a discussion or speaker has been, providing reasons for their opinions. Effective teacher questioning can support pupils to identify the strengths and areas for development of a particular speaker or discussion.

Alternatively, this task could be more closely guided by providing students with a checklist or prompt questions to aid their analysis of the clip. This could take the format of a talk detectives sheet. This approach can be particularly useful if you want to focus your class's attention on a specific skill or problem shown in the clip. For example, if students are not making eye contact with each other during discussions, this could be included in a checklist to complete while analyzing the clip, bringing their attention to this social and emotional element of discussion and prompting conversations as to why this is important.

FISH BOWL

A less technology-dependent way for students to critique each other's oracy is to use a "fishbowl." To set up a fishbowl, students need to be seated in two circles: a smaller inner circle and a larger outer circle. The students on the inner circle (the fish) engage in a discussion, while the students on the outer circle observe, providing feedback, when invited, on the oracy of those on the inner circle. Each member of the outer circle could be given a specific student or oracy skill to focus their observations on and guide their feedback.

A fishbowl focuses attention on listening skills, as the outer circle remains silent while listening in on the inner circle's discussion, providing the latter students ("the fish") with feedback at the end of their discussion. Be specific about exactly what you want the outer circle to be listening for. You could ask them to:

- Summarize what they have heard (possibly thematically) at the end of the discussion. This is cognitively demanding for members of the outer circle, who have to synthesize and condense what they have heard.
- Observe the inner circle with a focus on a specific strand of the Oracy Framework. For instance:

  o How well were people in the inner circle taking turns, inviting others in, and demonstrating listening (social and emotional)?
  o How did they use precise, carefully chosen language to highlight their expertise in this topic (linguistic)?
  o How did they develop their arguments and engage with the reasons offered by others (cognitive)?

o How well did they use their voice, facial expressions, and gestures to support the meaning of what they were saying (physical)?

Depending on how long you want the discussion to run, you could give the outer circle prompt sheets (talk detectives–style) to support their observations and feedback. Remember to swap the groups so that everyone has a chance to both speak and observe. You may want to have a different question or topic for the discussion the second time around.

MAKING TALK VISIBLE

It can be challenging for students to reflect on talk, as it is so intangible; they can't "see" it. It is easier to reflect on a piece of writing because it is in front of you and can be edited and revised. This is not the case with talk.

Filming discussion provides a record that can be analyzed. However, it can only be used *after* a discussion has taken place and does not support students to be reflective *during* the discussion. Providing students with physical representations to help them visualize talk can support them to be reflective during a discussion and to better understand the abstract components of talk. Making talk visible supports students to make conscious, strategic choices during a discussion.

A simple way to support students to manage their contributions in a discussion is to provide them with "talk tokens" to represent their contributions to a discussion. Students are given a set number of tokens, and once they have "spent" these they can no longer contribute to the discussion. This encourages students to carefully consider the volume and value of their contributions *during* a discussion. A more detailed description of this strategy and how it can help you create an inclusive classroom culture is provided in chapter 9.

TALK TOWERS

A sophisticated discussion is one in which students work toward a final shared understanding as participants build on each other's ideas. Less sophisticated discussions are characterized by a series of contributions that may be relevant but that do not engage with what has been said previously.

One method to help students to reflect on the quality of their discussions and the types of contributions they are making is to track them using Lego bricks. Each group is given a set of Lego bricks to represent each student's contribution to a discussion. After speaking, a student places a brick on the group's tower. However, if the contribution did not build on what has already been said, they must start a new tower to represent a new line of thought.

Generally, successful discussions will be shown by a few separate but developed towers. It would be clear if a group's discussion had been less successful, as their Lego bricks would show a scattering of undeveloped, individual towers. This would suggest that students had simply shared their own ideas rather than engaging with those of others. In contrast, a smaller number of more developed towers would suggest that students had explored several lines of inquiry, building on each other's ideas over the course of the discussion.

Developing students' metacognitive understanding and ability to reflect on talk enables them to think about talk as a process that can be improved and refined. Students can transfer their understanding of oracy to different contexts and subjects, as they have an understanding of what makes good talk, and a language to describe this, which can be applied in new and varied ways.

QUESTIONS TO CONSIDER

- How do your students know which talk skills are valued in your classroom?
- Do your students know how to improve the quality of their talk?
- Are your students able to identify and describe the elements of good talk?

NOTE

1. R. Evans and D. Jones, eds., *Metacognitive Approaches to Developing Oracy-Developing Speaking and Listening with Young Children* (New York: Routledge, 2008).

11

Create Authentic Contexts

A recent survey found that most people fear public speaking more than death,[1] which, as Jerry Seinfeld has joked, means the average person would rather be in the casket than giving the eulogy. While this statement may be a slight exaggeration, it is certainly true that for many people speaking in public can be an anxiety-inducing experience. Public speaking takes most people out of their comfort zone, leaving them uneasy or worried about how they will appear to others.

The angst or nervousness felt by many people in a public speaking scenario is not limited to situations in which they must speak in front of a large audience. Consider how nervous most people feel before a job interview where they must present their best self to an unfamiliar person or group of people. Or how nerve-racking it can be walking into and having to speak to a room of unfamiliar people in a personal or work context.

While there is no simple strategy to alleviate the anxiety or nerves arising from either of these scenarios, providing students with multiple and varied opportunities to speak in front of others, in a safe and supportive environment from a young age, can go a long way to reducing the fear felt by most people when speaking in unfamiliar situations.

The opportunities for talk outlined in this book so far have focused on how subject knowledge, thinking skills, and even vocabulary can be developed *through* talk. However, if our students are to become confident, agile communicators, we must provide them with opportunities to learn *how to talk* in a variety of contexts, speaking to a range of different audiences, and explicitly teach them the skills needed to do this successfully. Toward that end, it is useful to consider the purpose, context, and audience for talk in a given situation.

PURPOSE

How many times have you spoken today? You may have chatted with your children or family members at breakfast this morning, offered a greeting to the bus driver on the way into work, spoken to a group of colleagues during a meeting, given your food order to a server at lunchtime, and conversed with someone on the telephone.

What was the purpose of each of these conversations? To build relationships, to entertain, or to reach a consensus? Or was it more functional—to share information or to solve a problem? In each of these contexts, you will have altered your register, tone of voice, even your physical stance depending on the needs of the situation.

Every day as adults we are required to talk for a range of different purposes, adapting the way we speak in response to the purpose for which we are speaking. In most of these situations, we adapt our language, what we say, the way we hold ourselves, unthinkingly. However, we must not assume that our students can do the same without explicit instruction and plenty of practice.

Outlined below are a range of different purposes for talk. Consider the purpose of the different talk opportunities you provide for your students. Do they tend to fall under the same category? Or do you provide opportunities for pupils to talk for a variety of purposes? Do you explicitly teach them the skills required to do this?

- To problem solve
- To express yourself
- To challenge
- To entertain
- To influence
- To organize and structure ideas
- To acquire new language
- To understand and reason

- To analyze and evaluate
- To inform
- To generate ideas and opinions
- To build relationships
- To reach consensus or negotiate
- To gather and share information

Box 11.1 provides some insight as to how you might go about teaching students to talk for a specific purpose.

TALK TO BUILD RELATIONSHIPS

I wanted to spend some time building relationships with members of a new class, who were all new to the school and therefore did not know each other well. Talk is often a starting point for friendships and empathizing with others, yet it can be too easily dismissed as "chit-chat" and squeezed out of the classroom. In order to create a space for structured social talk, I developed a warm-up activity in which my students and I tried to work out an answer to the question "What is the best conversation starter ever?"

It works like this: In an open classroom space, students walk around in silence until they are given a signal—this could be a clap, a bell, or music stopping, musical statues–style. At the signal, they go to the person nearest to them and use a conversation starter. This could be something straightforward, like "What did you do this weekend?" or something more specific, like "What's your favorite car?" "Have you ever touched slime?" "What do you think of the president of the United States?"

The pair then have a conversation sprung from this question, before the other person asks their conversation starter. When the signal sounds again, they finish up what they are saying and return to walking around the room on their own—until the signal sounds again and the process is repeated.

Once everyone had a chance to mingle and strike up conversations with a number of peers, I stopped students and we spent some time identifying some of the best conversation starters and reflecting on why they were so effective. This required an awareness of the purpose of a conversation starter: to be interesting, entertaining, provocative, or thought-provoking. These ideas were then collated into a list we could refer back to in subsequent lessons, helping us continue our quest to find the best conversation starter ever!

—*Alice Stott*

CONTEXTS

Providing students with opportunities to speak in new and unfamiliar contexts is an excellent way to boost both student confidence and engagement. Selecting a presentational context for talk, such as creating a podcast or public service announcement, also provides pupils with opportunities to reinforce and deepen their subject knowledge. For example, if students have been learning about space and are then required to share this knowledge with others as part of a radio broadcast, they must be secure in their own understanding, developing and refining methods to share this understanding with others.

Existing classroom routines or school structures can be tweaked or adapted in order to provide students with opportunities to talk in varied contexts. For example, as part of a mathematics lesson, why not ask students to teach each other a method or concept? During school events, could students present instead of adults? When giving an achievement award, why not ask the students to stand up and explain why they have been nominated? Finally, when there are visitors at school, could your students become tour guides?

Listed below is a range of different contexts for talk. How many opportunities to talk in different contexts do you provide your students with currently?

Which could you incorporate into your teaching? What would be the purpose for talk in each of these context?

- Conversation
- Speech
- Interview
- Sports commentary
- Discussion
- Public service announcement
- Podcast
- Radio broadcast
- Tour guide
- Debate
- Storytelling
- Stand-up comedy
- Playing a game
- Teaching others
- Giving a presentation

AUDIENCES

Creating opportunities for students to talk to different audiences lifts talk beyond the classroom, raising the status of oracy. Speaking to an audience other than their teacher or peers raises expectations, encouraging students to improve the standard of their oracy. Consider, for example, the level of effort you would put into preparing and giving a presentation to a close group of peers compared to if you were delivering a presentation to an external panel of experts.

Of course, it is important to ensure that pupils have had adequate time to both prepare and practice before speaking to an audience, particularly if that audience is unfamiliar. However, providing students with opportunities to speak to a range of different audiences normalizes the experience, helping them to feel comfortable in what might otherwise be an uncomfortable situation. An example of how you can prepare your students to speak to an unfamiliar audience is set out in Box 11.2.

BOX 11.2

ORACY IN ACTION: PROGRESSION OF AUDIENCES

It is important to ensure that students are adequately prepared to speak in front of an unfamiliar audience. If students are unprepared or do not know how to be successful in a given situation, speaking in front of an unfamiliar audience can be a damaging rather than positive experience. It is therefore worth considering the progression of different audiences that students speak to before their final presentation or performance. Below is a suggested sequence of audiences that would support students to feel prepared speaking to an unfamiliar or large audience.

1. PAIRS
Once your students have had the opportunity to practice their presentation or speech independently and are familiar with what they are saying and how, the natural progression is practicing with a partner, who can prompt them if they forget what they are saying.

2. SMALL GROUPS
The next step is to provide pupils with the opportunity to present to a small group, in a more formal context. Trios are a good starting point. Ask two students to sit and listen while the third delivers all or elements of their speech or presentation. Students can then give each other feedback or critique on their presentations, focusing particularly on their delivery. This could be structured around a series of questions, such as: Was the speaker engaging? Did the speaker alter their physical stance or tone of voice? How did the speaker interact with the audience? Was the delivery clear and confident? Once students are confident presenting to this size group, you may want to increase the group size to six or larger.

3. THE REAL THING!
Before your students speak to the "real" audience, ensure that they are aware of how many people they will be speaking to and who the group is composed of. If speaking in an unfamiliar setting, such as a hall or auditorium, it is important to ensure that students have visited and practiced speaking in that setting before the final performance or presentation. If students are feeling particularly nervous, consider sitting at the front, in their eyeline, to act as a familiar, friendly face while they speak.

Outlined below is a range of different audiences. It is worth considering which is most appropriate for a given task or purpose. It is not always necessary to assemble a live audience; recording students speaking in a given context can be just as impactful, particularly if students are aware that the recording will be shared beyond the classroom.

- Peers
- Older
- Younger
- Large/small group
- Expert
- Live
- Recorded
- Familiar
- Unfamiliar

PLANNING FOR TALK OUTCOMES
Opportunities to speak for different purposes, in different contexts, for different audiences can and should be woven into lessons or sequences of learning. However, it is also beneficial, when possible, to plan for a specific talk outcome, carefully considering the purpose, context, and audience for talk and

explicitly teaching the skills necessary for this chosen outcome. To do this, think carefully about the subject content you are teaching and which context for talk this lends itself to.

For example, if teaching about antibiotic resistance in science, you could create a public service announcement (PSA) to warn people about the dangers of not completing a course of antibiotics. Next, consider what the purpose for talk would be in this context—for this example, to inform and to influence. Finally, think carefully about an appropriate audience for your students' output. In this case, a recorded presentation would work well, although it is worth considering how this could be shared with an authentic audience more widely.

Once you have decided on a purpose-context-audience combination, consider which skills your students will need to complete this assignment successfully. Use the four strands of the Oracy Framework to isolate individual skills. Table 11.1 outlines the skills required for a public service announcement.

It is important to share the success criteria for a given oracy outcome with students or, even better, to create this with them. For the example above, why not play students a number of different public service broadcasts and ask them to pick out the individual skills that sit under each strand? You could provide pupils with some prompt questions to discuss. For example: What is the purpose of the PSA? What tone of voice did the presenter use? What was

Table 11.1.

Context: a public service announcement	Purpose: to inform/to influence	Audience: unfamiliar, recorded
Oracy Skills		
Physical	• To speak clearly at an appropriate pace • To use a calm, reassuring tone of voice	
Cognitive	• To include relevant content (scientifically accurate yet accessible to the listener) • To follow the structure of a public service announcement (e.g., hook-example-problem-impact-call to action)	
Linguistic	• To use carefully chosen, well-explained vocabulary • To speak directly to the listener	
Social and Emotional	• To have audience awareness (an understanding of how you want the audience to feel when listening to the announcement—e.g., concerned and motivated, but not panicked)	

the impact of this on the listener? How did the PSA make you feel? What was the key information shared in the PSA? Why was this chosen?

Once you have created a set of shared success criteria with students for a given talk outcome, you then need to explicitly teach each of the skills. Each skill could be addressed briefly over the course of an individual lesson or focused on in more depth over a series of lessons.

Each different purpose-context-audience combination requires students to develop and practice different oracy skills. Over the course of their time at school, try to create opportunities for your students to talk for a range of different purposes, in different contexts, for different audiences. To ensure wide and varied coverage, it is worth keeping track of the different talk opportunities provided to students throughout their time at school.

QUESTIONS TO CONSIDER

- Do your students have opportunities to practice their oracy outside the classroom?
- How can you plan for talk outcomes across the curriculum?
- How can you use real-life audiences or contexts for talk to raise expectations for oracy?

NOTE

1. K. Burgess, "Speaking in Public Is Worse Than Death for Most," *The* (London) *Times*, October 30, 2013, https://www.thetimes.co.uk/article/speaking-in-public-is -worse-than-death-for-most-5l2bvqlmbnt. Accessed April 23, 2018.

12

Develop Oracy through Debate

Much of the rest of this book has focused on discussion skills. Typically, these involve teaching students to reach shared agreement through listening to one another, building on what has been previously said, and negotiating different points of view. However, there are plenty of reasons to bring disagreement, through debate, into your classroom.

Of course, some debates may end up happening spontaneously, for example, when students disagree within a discussion, and these challenges to each other's thinking should be encouraged, so long as they remain constructive and polite. This chapter focuses on how you can set up and teach the more formalized, presentational form of debating with fixed teams, set time limits for speeches, and clear roles.

WHY DEBATE?

Formalized debates bring to the fore a clash of points of view and competing arguments. As students have been allocated a side, the skill of debating comes down to *having* to think of arguments and counterarguments. This process forces students to engage with perspectives they may not have otherwise considered, and their opinion may shift or change as a result.

This is a direct contrast to a typical discussion, as shown in figure 12.1, where students have the space to explore their own opinions and contribute as and when they feel appropriate. Debate offers a different type of talk to

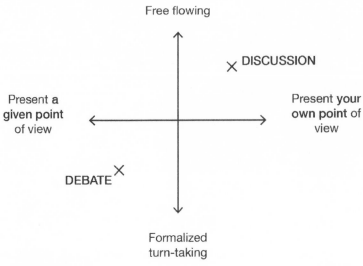

FIGURE 12.1
Discussion versus Debate

discussion: presentational rather than exploratory, structured rather than free flowing, prescribed rather than chosen lines of argument.

As a result, it is worth thinking carefully about the best moments to use debate in your classroom: Are there several strong sides of the argument to be explored? Would your students naturally tend to gravitate toward one point of view? Will your students have enough knowledge (of the topic, and of the world around them) to take into a debate?

Debate is also a great way to develop specific oracy skills, as shown in table 12.1. It is a highly cognitive exercise, but in order to successfully make powerful arguments, debaters must draw upon skills from all of the four strands.

Finally, debating brings with it competition. This can act as a powerful motivator for some students and provides a real purpose for having a well-developed line of argument: to win!

THE FORMAT

There are a huge range of debate formats out there, and it is worth exploring different setups with your students. It may be that you are already familiar with a certain format or style, as it mirrors the type of debate you see in your

Table 12.1.   Debate Judging Criteria Adapted from the Oracy Framework

Strand	Criteria	Marks Awarded

Physical	• Voice
	  —Fluency, clarity, voice projection, and tonal variation
	• Body Language
	  —Gesture and posture, eye contact
		5

Linguistic	• Vocabulary
	  —Deliberate vocabulary choices
	• Language
	  —Appropriate register
	• Rhetorical techniques
	  —Use of techniques for impact on audience
		5

Cognitive	• Content
	  —Choice of arguments and examples
	  —Building on the views of others
	• Structure
	  —Clear and deliberate organization of speech
	  —Strategic division of arguments within the team
	• Clarifying and summarizing
	  —Asking questions or making statements that undermine your opponent's case (Points of Information)
	  —Summarizing the debate as a whole
	• Self-regulation
	  —Maintaining focus on the debate (e.g., by offering Points of Information throughout)
	  —Managing time within the speech effectively
	• Reasoning and counterarguments
	  —Giving reasons to support views
	  —Critically examining ideas through rebuttal and Points of Information
		10

Social and Emotional	• Working with others
	  —Division of arguments within the team
	• Listening and responding appropriately
	  —Offering, accepting, and responding to POIs
	  —Rebuttal
	• Confidence in speaking
	  —Self-assurance
	  —Liveliness and flair
	• Audience awareness
	  —Framing speech to appeal to audience
		5

political or civic institutions. The format explained below is a modified version of the British Parliamentary debate format, which works well in class, as it has large teams and lots of opportunities for everyone to get involved.

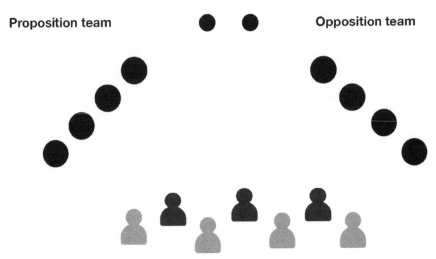

FIGURE 12.2
Debate Layout

The debate is set out as two opposing teams of four speakers each, as shown in figure 12.2. British Parliamentary debates would subdivide these into four teams of two, which creates internal competition between the first and second pair of speakers on each team. This additional challenge may work well with older students, but for simplicity having two teams of four works well.

There is also a chairperson, who introduces each speaker and organizes the floor debate; a timekeeper, who ensures that speakers run on time and that Points of Information (POIs) are only offered at the correct points; and an audience, who can contribute during the floor debate after the third opposition speaker has spoken.

Take the time needed to physically rearrange your classroom for each debate you have; it makes the whole process feel more real for your students and makes it easier to follow whose turn it is to speak next.

Once you have the basic layout, you then need to dig deeper into each of the speakers' roles within the debate. The best way to do this is to show your students a debate; this could be on TV, but even better is to have a show debate in class or in assembly. This could be modeled by more confident or experienced students, or teachers. Holding a show debate with teams made up of a mix of staff and students can go down really well, especially if the motion provides some room for humor!

If you choose to hold a show debate, carefully consider your choice of motion. It may be better to choose subject matter that is familiar or lighthearted so that students can focus on getting to grips with the roles within the debate, without having to simultaneously decipher unfamiliar arguments.

Each speaker in a debate has a specific role to fulfill, depending on where they are positioned in the debate. These roles are set out in brief in figure 12.3.

It can be useful to think about how the roles in the debate mirror those seen in the Houses of Parliament. The first proposition speaker is effectively the prime minister, proposing a motion or bill to Parliament. A motion is a statement that sets the topic for the debate, often starting with the phrase "This House would . . ." or "This House believes . . ." For example, "This House would levy a tax on sugary foods."

It is therefore imperative that the first proposition speaker defines exactly what is meant by the motion: any key terms that need explaining, thresholds that must be crossed, or sanctions that would need to be introduced. Much of the success of the debate will hinge on this definition; it needs to be a fair interpretation of the motion and enable both sides to build their cases in response to it. The first proposition speaker must then introduce the main thrust of their team's argument. This could include outlining problems with the status quo and giving reasons for the change they are proposing.

The first speaker for the opposition is equivalent to the leader of the opposition. Just as in Parliament, their role is to oppose the government's position. This should initially be through rebutting specific arguments made by the previous speaker, before introducing their team's central arguments.

It is then the turn of the second speaker for the proposition. Just like the deputy prime minister, their role is to attack the opposition's case and minimize any attacks made by the opposition against the prime minister's points, before introducing new arguments into the debate.

Similarly, the second speaker for the opposition, the deputy leader of the opposition, refutes the arguments made by the proposition, bolsters their own team's arguments, and then introduces their own new arguments.

The third speakers for each team can be thought of as backbench MPs or coalition partners: they rebut the other side's arguments and support their side, but perhaps have different reasons for doing so. In traditional British Parliamentary debates, their role is to add an "extension" to the debate: developing a new perspective or line of argument for their side.

1st proposition

Define the motion:
What do you want to change and why?
How will you make this change?
Introduce 2 or 3 main arguments.

2nd proposition

Rebut 1st opposition speaker's arguments. Introduce 2 or 3 main arguments.

3rd proposition

Rebut your opponents' arguments and rebuild you team's case. Introduce a new argument or angle to the debate.

Summary

Answer points from the floor debate. Summarize the debate as a whole. Do not introduce new points. What were the main arguments? How did your team win them?

Proposition team

1st opposition

Rebut the first speaker's case. Why are they wrong? Introduce 2 or 3 main arguments.

2nd opposition

Rebut 2nd Prop's arguments. Introduce 2 or 3 main arguments.

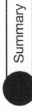

3rd opposition

Rebut your opponents' arguments and rebuild you team's case. Introduce a new argument or angle to the debate.

Summary

Answer points from the floor debate. Summarize the debate as a whole. What were the main arguments? How did your team win them?

Opposition team

FIGURE 12.3
Debate Speaker Roles

After the third speakers have each spoken, audience members have the chance to share their views in a "floor debate." The chairperson should organize the contributions and try to get a rough balance between points made for each side. Floor speakers might want to elaborate further on an argument already made in the debate, challenge a speaker, raise a point they think has been overlooked, or ask a question of one of the sides.

It is the summary speakers' job to respond to points made in the floor debate, and to summarize the debate as a whole. However, they are of course partisan—they can be thought of as the parliamentary whips for each side—and so each one's summary should favor their own side and make clear why their team has won the debate. You can maintain the alternation between speakers on each side, or you can swap the order and have the opposition summary followed by the proposition summary. This way, the proposition team gets the last word in the debate.

It can be a good idea to get a group of students up to sit in their debate positions and talk everyone through the running order and their roles by way of reminding them what they need to do. Think of it as commentating or narrating a debate, where you are able to press the "skip forward" button when needed.

Use your judgment as to how long each speech should last, depending on your students' confidence and experience at debating. In true British Parliamentary debates, each speech lasts up to seven minutes. However, you may want to start with shorter speeches, two to five minutes in length, increasing the time limit as students become more confident speaking at length.

Points of Information

There is one further, important layer that sits across every speaker's role in the debate. This is to offer and accept Points of Information. POIs are short (ten to fifteen seconds, maximum) interjections by the opposing team during a speech. The only exception to this are the summary speeches, where no POIs can be offered.

The purpose of a POI is to call attention to the weakness of the speaker's argument; this could be by asking a question, making a statement, or causing the speaker to return to a topic or idea they felt they had dealt with or had glossed over.

Anyone from the opposing team can offer a POI, and they must do so by standing up, putting out a hand, and saying clearly, "On a point of information," "On that point," or similar. See Box 12.1 for further detail on the exact physical stance needed to offer a POI.

It is then up to the speaker to decide whether to accept or decline the POI, or answer it in a moment. A speaker isn't obligated to accepted any POIs over the course of their speech, but if they turn down every one offered, they should be marked down for not engaging with the other team; it looks a bit like they are running scared! Equally, speakers who frequently offer POIs (whether accepted or not) or particularly pertinent POIs should be awarded by the judge for doing so.

For some students, standing up and interjecting can take some getting used to. A good POI is snappy and to the point. Similarly, when responding to a POI the speaker needs to think quickly, and be sharp and quick-witted in their reply. Spend some time practicing the skills specific to POIs as outlined in Box 12.2.

As POIs can disrupt a speaker's flow (indeed, that is often the intention), they cannot be offered in the opening and closing sections of a speech. This

---

BOX 12.1

ORACY IN ACTION: ACTING LIKE A DEBATER

The conventions for British Parliamentary debate extend beyond the linguistic to the physical, too. Originally, the House of Commons debating chamber was designed so that opposing parties would be seated or stood opposite each other, each behind a respective white line. The white lines marked the distance at which if either side were to draw out their swords, they would not be able to reach their opponents.

Similarly, when standing to offer a POI, the speaker should stand up with one hand behind their head and their other hand outstretched. Legend has it the hand behind the head was traditionally to enable the speaker to hold on to their wig, and the outstretched hand to show that they were not holding a sword! Why not get your students to offer their POIs as speakers hundreds of years ago in the Houses of Parliament would have done?

BOX 12.2

ORACY IN ACTION: PRACTICING POINTS OF INFORMATION

It can feel a little unnatural or unnerving to interrupt someone in front of an audience and so it's no surprise that POIs can take some time to get used to. One way to introduce them to your students is to set them up as a bit of a game.

Take one confident speaker (you would be a good first candidate, as someone they don't normally get the chance to interrupt!) and ask them to speak on a motion for a minute or two. This will work best if they are saying something likely to provoke a strong reaction from your class, so banning young people from doing things they enjoy (like eating sugar, or accessing the internet) may be a good place to start! While the speaker delivers their speech, the rest of the class can stand up to offer POIs. As in a debate, it is up to the speaker to decide whether to accept or decline each one. If they accept, they need to try to respond to the challenge raised and then continue with their speech until they accept another one.

You can play this for a number of rounds, swapping in new speakers. Aim to have every student in the class offer at least one POI, even if it is not accepted.

This game might also give you cause to teach your class what is meant by the term "barracking," when a speaker is relentlessly offered POIs by their opponents to the point of unfairness. Should your students inundate someone with POIs, explain to them that they must have a chance to deliver their speech and so POIs should be spaced out.

You may also want to highlight to students the need to be succinct and to the point for a POI. For anything said as a POI, the time is still running on the speaker's clock. It's therefore not fair to offer a long, waffling POI as you are taking time off the speaker. If someone does so, the speaker is allowed to cut them short and ask them to sit back down.

period is called "protected time," and it is usually the first and last minute of each speech. However, if your speeches are only three minutes in length, thirty seconds of protected time is more proportionate.

The end of protected time at the beginning of the speech, and the start of protected time at the end of the speech, should be signaled by the timekeeper knocking once on the table. This indicates to the other team that they are allowed to start offering POIs, or that they are out of time to do so. A double knock is typically used to indicate to a speaker when their time is up. If someone speaks well beyond their time, persistent gentle knocking until they wrap up usually does the trick!

KEY DEBATE SKILLS TO TEACH
Many of the oracy activities already discussed in this book will directly or indirectly support the skills needed for debate. More specifically, balloon debates, as outlined in Box 12.3, and opinion lines, as discussed in Box 12.4, are good activities to get students warmed up for a debate.

BOX 12.3

ORACY IN ACTION: BALLOON DEBATE

Imagine you are in a hot air balloon that is rapidly sinking. You are joined on board by a number of other passengers who are great figures from history, politics, and popular culture. The only solution, you all decide, is to throw someone overboard to try to stop the balloon sinking farther and avert disaster for everyone on board. This is the basic premise of a balloon debate, where the students take on a persona to represent and make the case for being allowed to remain on board the balloon, in order to be saved.

Start by giving students a bit of time to think about who they would like to become, for the purposes of the debate. Try letting your students choose anyone who they think they can make a strong case for; they will need to consider whether they know enough about this person to speak on their behalf. You could end up with figures from history, from fiction, from current affairs, or from real life, such as a student's mum.

Alternatively, you could set a theme or allocate specific characters to your students. To help students to prepare, you may want to put students into small groups, with each group putting forward one person to represent them.

Aim to have about six speakers in the debate, with the rest of the class as the audience, responsible for deciding whom to jettison and whom to save. Give each speaker a fair amount of time to introduce who they are and make their case—normally thirty seconds or a minute works well. In that time, they need to explain who they are and why they deserve to remain in the hot air balloon.

Once each speaker has spoken, the audience members have their chance to vote to decide who should remain in the balloon. Remind them that they are acting as judges, not just choosing who they like the most (real or imagined!). Instead, they should think about who made the most convincing case for the persona they represent. The person with the lowest number of votes is eliminated and joins the audience.

In subsequent rounds, the speakers have the advantage of having heard what each other has said. This enables them to rebut each other's arguments—not only making their case but also trying to erode the legitimacy of their fellow balloon passengers. After each round of speeches, the audience casts a vote to decide whom to save (the balloon keeps sinking!). In later rounds, you may want to involve the audience in putting questions to each of the remaining speakers. The number of passengers in the balloon dwindles until the two final speakers go head-to-head in a final round to decide who will be saved!

Debating requires students to employ a range of different skills in order to create a coherent case. Below are some of the specific skills that you may want to build up with your students through debating and some ideas on how to do so.

BOX 12.4

ORACY IN ACTION: OPINION LINES

Introduce your students to the idea that the room you are in represents a continuum of different opinions: from very strongly agree at one end to very strongly disagree at the other, and every other shade of (dis)agreement or indecision in between.

Give your students a statement or motion, such as "This House would introduce compulsory military service." Allow your students a moment to think about where they would place themselves on the opinion line—they need to get up and stand in the spot that corresponds to their point of view. If they are undecided, they can remain in the middle but they will need to be ready to explain why they have remained on the fence.

After the students have found their positions, find out why they have chosen to stand where they are. Garner a couple of different opinions to compare, and as you do encourage everyone else to move if they hear something that makes them change their mind—changing their position on the continuum. Can a student explain their stance, and with the power of their argument move more of their peers to the side with their point of view?

Once you have explored one motion or issue, introduce a new one and start the process over again.

Generating and Organizing Arguments

Your students will need to become adept at arguing, able to empathize with alternative perspectives, and able to generate lots of different reasons for a particular side. Teach them to do this by jointly planning a couple of debates, modeling how a teacher might approach preparing for a debate. This could follow a process like:

1. Check as a team that we all understand what the motion means.
2. Create a list of our first instinct points for our side—as many ideas as possible without a view to deciding which are strongest, yet.

3. Add to our list of points by systematically going through all the people/ groups who would be directly or indirectly affected by the motion. Are there any groups who need particular consideration? How would we "sell" the issue to them?

4. As a group, prioritize the case by working out which are the biggest, most important arguments. These will need to be made by the first and second speakers. Is there a natural way of dividing up arguments between speakers? How can the third speaker build on what the first speakers say—is there something new or different they can add?

5. Ensure that the first three speakers have at least one, ideally two or three, meaty arguments they can make. Emphasize that students will win or lose as a *team*, not individual speakers; they must ensure that everyone in the team fulfills their role in the debate.

6. If you are able to, come up with a central line of argument that will run through all the speeches made by your team like a red thread. (Think of it like an essay, where each paragraph makes a different point but contributes to the essay's central thesis in some way.) The first speaker can set up this central narrative for the team, with subsequent speakers returning to it and reinforcing it.

Developing Arguments

When asked to stand up and deliver their speech, some students resort to simply listing a set of reasons for their side. To be successful, they need to have just two or three arguments that are well-explained, developed, and clearly linked to their side of the debate.

One of the best ways to get students to develop their points is to encourage them to use examples. These could be real (from the news, or from their own lives) or hypothetical. These examples must be clearly linked to the motion at hand, and analyzed carefully in relation to the debate. A handy mnemonic to remind students to do this is PEE: point, evidence, explain. The example set out in table 12.2 is for a debate about the death penalty.

It is often the final stage of "explaining" that students skip, or do not spend enough time on. To be successful, they need to really spell out for their audience the logical steps in their argument: if X then Y; if X then Y but also Z, then is Y still desirable?; or X won't lead to desired outcome of Y.

Table 12.2. Point, Evidence, Explain

Point	One of the main reasons stated in favor of the death penalty is that it will act as a deterrent; however, this is not the case.
Evidence	Take, for example, a murderer who killed in a fit of rage with no premeditation. They simply "lost it" and on the spur of the moment went too far in a fight.
Explain	Lots of murders are not planned, and the people committing them do not think of the consequences of their actions. The proposal of the death penalty does not lead to the desired outcome, of a reduction in the number of murders. Therefore there is no grounds to support the death penalty.

Talking Like a Debater

For many students, one of the joys of debating is that it brings with it its own language and ways of speaking. This can feel a bit like getting into role, becoming a politician, rather than just being yourself, which can help with confidence.

Have a go at introducing your students to some of the sentence stems and phrases in table 12.3—they may love adopting some of the formalities and traditions associated with British parliamentary debating!

Generating Rebuttal

Another important debate skill is being able to make clear counterarguments through rebuttal. Once the speaker has introduced their points ("Today, I'm going to make three main points, which are . . .") they should spend some time rebutting what has been said by the previous speaker ("Before I start on my first point, I would like to rebut some of the arguments made by the previous speaker . . .").

In order to do a good job of rebutting what has been said, students need to understand what they are trying to achieve. You might want to use an analogy. Each team in the debate is trying to build up their argument; imagine they are building a tower. They will build a strong tower if their arguments are strong. However, to win, they also need to knock down their opponents' tower—by removing individual blocks or, if they can, attacking the foundations on which the whole tower rests.

For some students rebuttal can be challenging, as it requires spontaneously generating counterarguments. Also, some students fall into the trap of focusing their rebuttal on a relatively minor point in the debate rather than attacking the foundations of their opponent's argument. Encourage your students to take on their opponent's biggest arguments, prioritizing these in order to discredit their central argument!

Table 12.3. Sentence Stems and Phrases to Talk Like a Debater

To chair the debate	• Ladies and gentlemen, please welcome to the floor (name), to open the case for the proposition/opposition. • I thank the speaker for their speech, and would now like to introduce (name), to speak for the proposition/opposition. • I would now like to open the debate up to the floor. Please indicate if you would like to speak. • Finally, to summarize for the proposition/opposition, we welcome (name)!
To introduce a point	• On the proposition/opposition, we stand for . . . • Our central argument is . . . • My first/second/third point is . . . • Now this brings me on to my next point, which is . . .
To rebut a point	• The opposition think that . . . However, . . . • The previous speaker said . . . but they have not answered our point that . . . • In order to win this debate, the other side needs to prove to you that . . . They have not done this because . . . • What the other team has failed to consider is . . . • The other side has told you about X. However, what they haven't told you about is Y . . . • Our side has been making the point that . . . and the only response the opposition has offered is . . .
To offer a point of information	• On a point of information . . . • On that point . . . • POI? • Sir/Madam?
To accept a point of information	• Accepted • Go ahead • One moment please
To decline a point of information (this must always be polite!)	• No, thank you • Declined • Not right now, thank you
To conclude your speech	• Finally, to summarize what I have told you today . . . • So, what have I told you today? My three main points were . . . • I want to leave you with one final thought today, which is . . . • Just to conclude my speech, let me return to my main points, which were . . . It is for these reasons that I am proud to stand with the proposition/opposition!

Summarizing

Summarizing is a crucial skill in debating, as it is one of the best ways to get the audience (and judges!) to remember what you have said. Encourage your students to clearly flag the structure of their speech: "Say what you are going to say, say it, and then say what you have said." The simplest way for your students to do this is to outline the two or three main arguments they will make at the start of their speech, and return to these at the end of the speech.

As the name suggests, the summary speaker for each team must try to summarize the debate as a whole. In order to do so, they should not introduce any new points, although they may want to respond to points raised in the floor debate and/or offer some rebuttal. The best summary speakers will weave rebuttal into their speech as part of their summary.

In order to summarize the debate, the summary speaker should listen carefully to both sides in the debate and keep notes on each speaker. This will help them to formulate their summary—which they will need to do while the debate is in session.

There are a number of ways a summary speech can be structured. It could be done by looking at the main points of clash in the debate, setting out what each side said on each issue, and showing how the summary speaker's team made the most compelling case on each point of clash. Alternatively, they could summarize the debate speaker by speaker, again highlighting how their team made the strongest points.

Crucially, however a summary speaker chooses to structure their speech, they need to paint the debate as one their team clearly won. It can be useful to explain this to students as being like giving a biased news report: you need to relay what has happened but with a clear point of view.

Talking Up Your Team

The social and emotional strand is important in a debate. Not only is it important to consider your audience and judges, and how you can have the greatest impact on them, but also how you work together as a team.

Emphasize to your students that they will win, or lose, as a team. How they work together to prepare for the debate, and how they support each other once it has started, will certainly influence the outcome of the debate. Successful debate teams share out arguments, help each other to come up with points or examples, and ensure everyone's voice is heard during preparation time so that everyone in the team enters the debate feeling confident.

Similarly, during a debate, students should act as a team. They need to back up the points made by other speakers on their side if they come under attack in rebuttal, remind the audience what their other team members have said or are going to say, and offer POIs that aid their side, not just their individual case. The summary speaker in particular has a big role to play in talking up their team and emphasizing that the best points in the debate have come from their side.

JUDGING

British parliamentary debates are normally judged for content (the strength of arguments), strategy (the decisions taken by the team about how to deliver their arguments and use POIs), and style (the speaking style and confidence of the speaker). These can be mapped onto the Oracy Framework, which can be adapted to provide a judging criteria for a debate, as shown earlier in table 12.1.

Each speaker is marked out of 25 points, with a double weighting accorded to the cognitive strand, as this is the most important in a debate. Each team of four speakers therefore gets a total mark out of 100. It can also be useful to keep a tally of POIs offered and accepted by each speaker, to track their participation in the debate. For example, if the first speaker delivers their speech and then effectively tunes out of the rest of the debate and doesn't offer any POIs, they should be marked down on the social and emotional strand.

TO PREP OR NOT TO PREP

You have a choice as to whether to do a prepared motion, where students know the motion in advance and can do research and construct their arguments ahead of the debate, or an unseen motion, where students have only fifteen minutes to pull together their case before the debate starts.

Each has its own advantages. A prepared debate requires students to seek out knowledge, information, and arguments—and gives them a clear purpose for doing so. On the other hand, an unseen motion demands that students think spontaneously and apply their knowledge of argumentation and debate to the issue at hand. A middle ground could be forewarning students as to the debate topic, but providing the motion and allocating sides with just fifteen minutes' notice.

If you do choose to give students unseen motions, guide them to put their preparation time to good use. A good balance is half the time spent thinking and planning collectively as a team, followed by the rest of the time working through their case and writing up notes independently.

In neither prepared nor unseen debates should students be encouraged to write out speeches in full sentences. This stilts delivery and often makes students dependent on a speech that may have been made redundant earlier in the debate. Instead, encourage them to write clear notes, which they can use to support their fluent delivery.

Although it may take some time to familiarize your students with the conventions of debate, once they have grasped the basics it is a great way to introduce structured disagreement into your classroom. The formulaic nature of debating provides a framework through which students can interrogate arguments, explore different subject matter, and challenge each other's thinking.

QUESTIONS TO CONSIDER
- How can you introduce your students to the format of a debate?
- Which skills will you teach as part of debating?
- Which motions are likely to provoke a passionate response from your students?

Make Meaningful Use of Assessment

Assessment of oracy is a thorny issue, and—full disclosure—is needed right away. This chapter is not going to give you one single, definitive answer as to how you should go about assessing the oracy of the children you teach. It will, however, introduce you to a number of approaches for formatively assessing oracy and explore some of the big questions and challenges that underlie summative assessment of oracy.

WHY ASSESS ORACY?

The first question that needs exploring is, why does assessment matter for oracy? It matters because to know *what* to assess requires us to know what it is we are looking for, and to define what "good" looks like. In this way, assessment brings with it a shared standard and common understanding of the oracy skills students should have, at a certain age, and at a certain level.

This common understanding of what "good" looks like feeds directly into what happens in classrooms every day. If you have a benchmark or set of standards against which to assess oracy, you can gauge what your students have or have not yet grasped and know what to teach next, or what to re-teach. This process of formative assessment, where information gathered from assessment is used to adapt teaching in direct response to the needs of the students,[1] makes us better, more precise teachers. This is as true for oracy teaching and learning as it is for any other subject or skill.

Moreover, what is assessed tends to be what gets taught. In this regard, assessments and tests often provide the educational equivalent of a bottom line, a measure of the skills and knowledge deemed essential for every child to have acquired on their journey through school. If oracy is assessed, the implication is that it is important: the skills are worth having and measuring.

If, therefore, we accept that assessment of oracy is important, this leads us to ask what kind of oracy assessment is best. The answer generally depends on the audience for whom the information is intended and what it will be used for. Consider the following audiences and what they would use assessment for:

1. Children: to know what they are doing well at and how to improve further.
2. Teachers: to assess an individual child's progress over time (and intervene or make changes in response to this data and to differentiate accordingly); to make comparisons between students, classes, and cohorts.
3. Parents/caregivers: to understand their child's progress and how to better support them.
4. Stakeholders within the wider education system: to monitor school performance and make comparisons between outcomes in different cohorts, schools, or education systems.

There are a range of assessment methods to gather the information needed to fulfill points one to three, many of them oracy-specific adaptations of typical formative assessment for learning strategies. It is the fourth and final point that presents the most difficulty, as the challenges in assessing oracy are made particularly acute when the purpose of assessment is to provide a single summative oracy "grade" for an audience "external" to your classroom, to enable comparisons between schools and across the education system.

FORMATIVE ASSESSMENT IN ORACY
It is highly likely that you are already making judgments and implicitly assessing the oracy of students in your classroom. You may well have identified quieter students and introduced strategies to create opportunities for them

to speak up or given feedback to a child who has a tendency to dominate a discussion. You are likely aware of which students will happily talk at length in front of an audience and those for whom such an experience would be anxiety-inducing.

This type of observation and assessment of oracy can be built upon by using the Oracy Framework, which provides a balanced and systematic lens through which you can identify your students' strengths and areas for development.

ORACY ASSESSMENT FOR LEARNING STRATEGIES

Get Instant Feedback

Ask your students to signal how their discussion went and use this to judge whether to give the class more time or whether to wrap things up. For instance, you could pause a discussion to ask students to put their hand up if they have yet to speak, or give you a thumbs-up if they have reached shared agreement or invited someone else into the discussion.

Another option is to use finger scales, on a scale of one to five. Ask students to rate their response to various questions: How confident were you speaking? How well did your partner listen to you? How much did you contribute to your discussion? This can provide a good starting point for students to consider how they can improve: for example, if you were only listening at a three out of five today, what would a five out of five look like?

Success Criteria

Create oracy-specific success criteria. These could be specific to the type of talk or context your students are learning about, as seen in figure 13.1, which is for a speech, or figure 13.2, which is for storytelling. It may be that you want to focus on a couple of core skills, or put the spotlight on one or two strands of the Oracy Framework that you particularly want to develop—for instance, focusing on the physical and social and emotional aspects of group talk, as shown in table 13.1.

Oracy Expert Observer

Name of observer: Name of speaker:

Strand	Tick all statements that apply to the speaker	Further notes
PHYSICAL	☐ Varies their voice (tone, volume, pace, pauses) for effect. ☐ Uses hand gestures and facial expressions to support what they are saying. ☐ Uses the space confidently (e.g., comes forward to the audience).	
LINGUISTIC	☐ Uses unusual, powerful, or emotive language. ☐ Uses rhetorical devices (e.g., rhetorical questions, metaphors, lists of three).	
COGNITIVE	☐ Has chosen a topic they are able to talk about in detail and in depth. ☐ Gives developed reasons for their opinions. ☐ Structures their speech clearly (e.g., a beginning, middle, and end; a circular structure which returns to an idea from the start).	
SOCIAL & EMOTIONAL	☐ Makes a connection with their audience (e.g., by hooking them, by linking to their shared experiences). ☐ Speaks with confidence (e.g., makes strong eye contact).	

Overall comments:

The strengths of this speech were:

What would have made this speech even better?

FIGURE 13.1
Speech Success Criteria

To use an expressive voice
To use gestures/props

 To use prepositional time and place phrases
To use transition phrases typical to the oral tradition

 To tell your story using a logical sequence

 To make eye contact with your audience
To make your audience feel excited

FIGURE 13.2
Storytelling Success Criteria

Table 13.1. Social and Emotional Success Criteria

Invite others in	Ask questions, say someone's name, or gesture to them
Demonstrate listening	Make eye contact and have still and focused body language
"Share the air"	Take turns, making sure everyone in the group has the opportunity to speak

On the other hand, you might want your success criteria to remain consistent over the course of the year, particularly if you are focusing on improving a specific type of talk. Discussion guidelines or ground rules for talk, outlined in chapter 3, are an example of where there is benefit in keeping the success criteria constant, even as the subject matter for discussion changes across the year. The Listening Ladder, outlined in chapter 8, is a set of success criteria specifically for listening, which can also be kept constant throughout the year.

Another option is to co-construct your success criteria with your students by looking at several different examples for the type of talk they are learning about and drawing out the skills involved. This is a useful exercise if you want to set clear, high expectations for oracy with students at the start of a project. It also works well if there are several different styles or ways of delivering an outcome that you want to show to students—their task becomes to spot the commonalities between each speaker.

Once you have created success criteria, make them explicit to students, model them, and create time in lessons for students to reflect on to what extent they, or one of their classmates, met them. This could be done by referring back to the success criteria and color-coding them (red/amber/green) or noting down observations against them as someone is speaking.

Set Targets

Set oracy-specific targets, share them with your students and their parents/caregivers, and periodically review your students' progress against them. Alternatively, get students to set their own targets or targets for their peers and monitor their own progress against them. You may need to support students to do this—for instance, by providing a target bank from which they can select their personal targets. An example is set out in table 13.2.

Table 13.2. Target Bank

- To speak loudly and clearly, and to pause to allow my audience to think about what I am saying
- To use technical vocabulary that shows my expertise
- To develop my opinions by giving examples and reasons for what I think
- To listen to what others say, and ask questions to help clarify my own and others' understanding
- To politely challenge others' points of view by offering alternative opinions or asking probing questions
- To be confident about my ideas and to show this by making eye contact with my listeners
- To think carefully about how much I have contributed compared to others in the group
- To try to balance my contributions with others'

Track Progress

Create systems to track your students' progress in oracy. Use the knowledge you have built up through observing students in your classroom to color-code them red/amber/green against each of the four strands (or the most pertinent criteria you choose) to get a sense of where students in your class are, relative to each other. This will enable you to think about their strengths and areas for development at a cohort level. For instance, on which of the four strands is your class strongest and on which are they weakest? Is there a difference between boys and girls? How do their oracy skills change and develop over the year?

Alternatively, you could track the number and types of extended contributions made by students in small-group or whole-class discussions. For instance, you could keep a note of how many times each student has contributed, asked a question, or challenged someone else's point of view. You might want to make this process transparent to the students and get them involved in helping you to track the different contributions, and in doing so raise their awareness of the types of contributions you value.

Box 13.1 and figure 13.3 provide examples of a Harkness discussion tracking tool, which shows the number and nature of contributions made by different students in a group. The visual representation of the discussion often

BOX 13.1

ORACY IN ACTION: HARKNESS DISCUSSIONS

On April 9, 1930, American philanthropist Edward Harkness wrote to Phillip Exeter Academy's principal, Lewis Perry, regarding how a considerable donation he had made to the academy might be used: "What I have in mind is [a classroom] where [students] could sit around a table with a teacher who would talk with them and instruct them by a sort of tutorial or conference method, where [each student] would feel encouraged to speak up. This would be a real revolution in methods."

The result, championed by Phillips Exeter Academy, New Hampshire, is the Harkness discussion: twelve students sit around an oval table and engage in free-flowing, open, collaborative discussion on the subject at hand, guided by their teacher.

As part of a Harkness discussion, the contributions made by students are tracked visually, and a key records the nature of the contribution. This provides a record of the discussion and enables the participants to see how their contributions fit into the wider discussion and to reflect on their role in moving the group's knowledge and understanding forward.

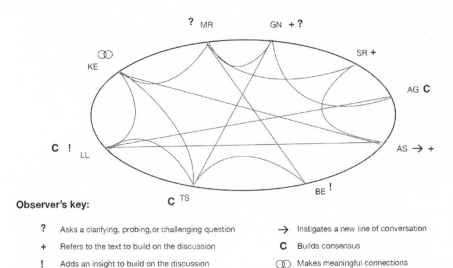

Observer's key:

?	Asks a clarifying, probing, or challenging question	→	Instigates a new line of conversation
+	Refers to the text to build on the discussion	C	Builds consensus
!	Adds an insight to build on the discussion	⊂⊃	Makes meaningful connections

FIGURE 13.3
Harkness Discussion Tracking Tool

encourages students to be reflective about their contributions, and it can be interesting to compare trackers from different discussions over the course of the year to see how the spread of contributions has changed. Also, the role of discussion tracker can be a good one for students who may otherwise dominate a discussion!

Assess Subject Knowledge through Talk

Create opportunities to assess subject knowledge through talk—and assess talk at the same time. Classroom discussion and student responses to questions are valuable assessment for learning (AFL) strategies in and of themselves, but remember that you can also use them as opportunities to assess your students' oracy. You can learn a lot about their level of understanding not only from *what* they say, but also *how* they say it. For instance, are they using the precise terminology needed? The appropriate level of formality? Have they organized their answer logically? Can they respond to a question or challenge from a peer?

THE CHALLENGES OF SUMMATIVE ASSESSMENT

All of the assessment tools outlined above help you as a teacher, your students, and their parents/caregivers to know what a child is doing well, and how they can improve further in oracy. However, they don't meet the needs of the fourth and final reason to assess: to enable us to make comparisons between schools and education systems.

While there are some exams that offer this type of assessment, it is difficult to point to any model as perfect. Devising a method to summatively assess oracy—which would enable us to ascribe a grade, number, or level that could stand the test of time, enabling us to make comparisons between students in different schools or even countries—is tricky. It's hard to create an oracy assessment model that is "fair," let alone perfect, for a number of reasons.

Context Matters

How well a child will perform in any given situation depends on a whole host of other factors beyond just their ability to communicate through speaking and listening. Students may well perform differently depending on the subject matter they are required to talk about, the context or setting in which they are speaking, and indeed who they are talking to. For these reasons, it is very difficult to create a context for assessment that is "fair" and gives an equal chance of success to all students involved.

The Type of Talk Matters

Looking beyond the subject matter and the context that students are assessed in, there comes a further challenge: How do you design a set of balanced assessment tasks?

Most speaking and listening assessments evaluate a final, polished piece of presentational talk such as a presentation or speech, which may be followed up with some questions. However, to use this as the only measure of students' oracy skews what is being assessed (and therefore what tends to be valued) in favor of individual, presentational talk at the expense of collaborative, exploratory talk.

Subtlety and Subjectivity

A further challenge stems from the subtlety and subjectivity of talk. It goes without saying that what makes someone a strong speaker is very subjective. One person's idea of good listening and patient turn-taking might be seen by another as reticence. What one might see as powerful and passionate delivery, another might see as forceful and overbearing. How should we score the single contribution made by a quieter student, if it actually turns out to be the most incisive in the whole discussion?

Logistical Challenges

Finally, there are also plenty of logistical reasons why summatively assessing oracy is complicated. Finding the time, the staff, the space, and the recording equipment (if needed) to assess every student can be a real challenge for most schools. There isn't a quick fix as to how to get around the heavy resource investment needed to do a thorough job, and so it may be worth considering whether you need to assess every single child, or whether a "tracker" sample will give you much of the information that you need.

THE ORACY ASSESSMENT TOOLKIT

It may well feel at this point that there is little hope, then, for a sound oracy assessment model. In an ideal world, an oracy assessment would triangulate multiple data points to create an impression of a student's ability: in different contexts; on a range of subject matter; engaging in different types of talk, rather than hinging on a single snapshot from one task. It would capture a number of different assessors' opinions and balance them against each other. And it would all be done using minimal resources!

That said, Voice 21 has developed a summative assessment model, drawing on the Oracy Assessment Toolkit created by Cambridge University,[2] which goes some way to addressing the challenges specific to oracy assessment. It is outlined in Box 13.2.

BOX 13.2

ORACY IN ACTION: ASSESSING ORACY

As part of a pilot exploring the impact of an oracy curriculum on a year group, Voice 21 devised an assessment system that was based on the Cambridge Oracy Assessment Toolkit.[1] Two different tasks highlight different areas of the Oracy Framework, outlined in table 13.3 and table 13.4.

Table 13.3. Talking Points Task Criteria

Physical

Voice	• Uses variations in emphasis, pace, volume, and pitch to enhance the meaning of their speech • Pronounces words with clarity and precision • Speaks at a volume appropriate for the situation
Body Language	• Uses appropriate gestures and posture to convey and enhance the meaning of their speech • Uses appropriate facial expressions and eye contact to enhance the meaning of their speech and to engage with others

Linguistic

Grammar and Register	• Uses correct grammar • Uses a register appropriate to the purpose and context
Rhetoric and Vocabulary	• Uses apt and varied vocabulary, including appropriate and accurate use of relevant technical terms • Uses devices such as metaphor, simile, anecdote, and jokes to enhance the meaning of their speech

Cognitive

Content and Reasoning	• Exercises judgment over what content is relevant and interesting, given the particular situation, in order to convey meaning and intention • Is able to explain and justify their points of view clearly
Building on Views of Others and Critical Examination	• Develops, challenges, and critiques the ideas of others by adding to their argument and/or testing and questioning the rationale of their argument

Social and Emotional

Turn-Taking, Guiding and Managing Interactions	• Acts sensitively in taking turns and allows sufficient opportunities for others to do so • Enables conversation, discussion, or debate to continue by making appropriate contributions and encouraging others to contribute
Active Listening	• Demonstrates that they are attending and listening to what other speakers have said

Table 13.4. Presentation Task Criteria

Physical

Voice	• Allows listeners sufficient time to process what is said and avoids excessive pausing or hesitation • Uses variations in emphasis, volume, and pitch to enhance the meaning of their speech • Pronounces words with clarity and precision, without muttering or slurring • Speaks loudly enough to suit the needs of the situation
Body Language	• Uses appropriate gestures and posture to convey and enhance the meaning of their speech and engagement with audience • Uses appropriate facial expressions and eye contact to enhance the meaning of their speech and engagement with audience

Linguistic

Vocabulary and Rhetoric	• Uses apt and varied vocabulary, including appropriate and accurate use of relevant technical terms • Uses devices such as metaphor, simile, anecdote, and jokes to enhance the meaning of their speech
Register and Grammar	• Uses correct grammar • Uses language appropriate for the purpose and context

Cognitive

Content and Reasoning	• Exercises judgment over what content is relevant and interesting • Is able to explain and justify their points of view clearly and effectively in words • Takes account of level of understanding of the audience
Structure and Self-Regulation	• Selects and organizes the content of their talk so that it is relevant, clear, and comprehensible to listeners • Keeps focused and on-task, managing to link points together to develop a coherent argument and narrative

Social and Emotional

Confidence and Flair	• Manages their nervousness and demonstrates self-assurance in performance • Shows enthusiasm and imagination to achieve a distinctive and effective use of talk
Audience Awareness and Engagement	• Develops rapport with the audience • Judges what listeners already know about the topic and is able to empathize with their audience

The first task is a "talking points" discussion, in groups of three, which creates a forum for spontaneous, exploratory group talk and requires students to listen to each other and manage interactions. The second is a presentation task, where students are asked to give a one-minute presentation "to camera" to be shared with a specific audience. This creates a context for prepared, presentational, individual talk, and as there is a specified audience, students must also demonstrate audience awareness.

The subject matter is designed to be as open and accessible as possible; something they are likely to be able to talk about. For each talking points task, the statements are themed around a topic such as money or animals. Students are given a number of talking points to discuss. They can choose, as a group, from the list of talking points depending on what interests them the most. Below are some examples on the topic of money:

1. Money does not make people happy.
2. Some people, like football players, get paid too much.
3. There is never a good reason to steal money.
4. People should get the same pay whatever job they do.
5. Rich people are greedy; poor people are lazy.

Students are given about six to eight minutes, in their trios, to discuss the talking points. They are free to spend all their time on one, if it particularly interests them, or to move on to another talking point.

For the presentation task, the subject is again selected to feel relevant to all students and to ensure their presentations have a clearly specified audience. Students complete one presentation task at each assessment point. Presentation tasks could include:

- Give a one-minute presentation to camera on the topic of "how to settle in at a new school," which will be shown to younger students about to move schools.

- Give a one-minute speech to camera for prospective parents explaining why they should choose to send their child to this school.

- Give a one-minute speech to camera on the topic "how this school could be improved" to be shown to your teachers at your school.

Students are given ten minutes to prepare before being filmed giving their presentations. If a student struggles to speak for an extended period of time, ask them prompt questions and give them encouragement.

In terms of the actual marking and grading process, the mark sheets have been designed to be as simple as possible, so that teachers can mark students "live," in the moment. However, it is much easier to mark (as well as standardize and moderate) using recordings of students, which enables you to rewatch clips and discuss them. Figure 13.4 is the talking points task mark sheet, which captures the scores for the three students in the discussion; figure 13.5 is the individual presentation task mark sheet.

For each task, there are eight criteria students are marked against: two for each strand of the framework. As shown in figure 13.4, figure 13.5, and table 13.5, students can be awarded a mark of 0 to 3 for each criteria.

This gives a total mark of 24 for each task, totaling 48 overall. Score ranges are broken down into the bands shown in table 13.6 to describe student attainment. This process can be done at two or three intervals over the year to try to quantify changes in students' oracy skills.

Although this assessment process has been designed in an attempt to iron out some of the summative assessment challenges outlined previously, it still isn't perfect. In particular, there is a challenge around adjusting expectations for students' age (how does competent use of a skill look different at age eight versus eighteen?) and how to account for any "natural" progression that may have come about regardless of the oracy teaching that has taken place.

Task: Student-led Talking Point discussion
Title: Choice of talking points from list
Grouping: Three students in each group

0. Student demonstrates no evidence of skill
1. Student demonstrates limited signs of skill but not intentionally or effectively
2. Student demonstrates some signs of purposeful and effective use of this skill
3. Student is clearly and competently using this skill purposefully, naturally, & effectively

Name of assessor:
Student name/identifier:

	0	1	2	3	Notes
Physical					
Voice					
Body language					
Linguistic					
Vocabulary & Rhetoric					
Grammar & register					
Cognitive					
Content & Reasoning					
Building on views of others, summarizing & critically examining					
Social & Emotional					
Turn taking, guiding & managing interactions					
Active listening					

FIGURE 13.4
Talking Points Assessment Task Mark Sheet

Task: One-minute presentation "to camera"
Title: Choice of presentation topic
Audience: Choice of audience relevant to the topic

0. Student demonstrates no evidence of skill
1. Student demonstrates limited signs of skill but not intentionally or effectively
2. Student demonstrates some signs of purposeful and effective use of skill
3. Students is clearly and competently using this skill purposefully, naturally, & effectively

Name of assessor:
Student name/identifier:

	0	1	2	3	Notes
Physical					
Voice					
Body language					
Linguistic					
Vocabulary & Rhetoric					
Grammar & register					
Cognitive					
Content & Reasoning					
Structure & self-regulation					
Social & Emotional					
Confidence & flair					
Audience awareness					

FIGURE 13.5
Presentation Assessment Task Mark Sheet

Table 13.5. Marking Criteria

0	Foundation	Student demonstrates no evidence of skill
1	Beginner	Student demonstrates limited signs of skill but it may not be intentional or effective or support the purpose
2	Developer	Student demonstrates some signs of purposeful and effective use of this skill
3	Confident	Student clearly and competently uses this skill purposefully, naturally, and effectively

Table 13.6. Assessment Bands

	Band Descriptor	Marks
1	Foundation—Emerging	1–6
2	Foundation—Secure	7–12
3	Beginner—Emerging	13–18
4	Beginner—Secure	19–24
5	Developer—Emerging	25–30
6	Developer—Secure	31–36
7	Confident—Emerging	37–42
8	Confident—Secure	43–48

NOTE

1. N. Mercer, P. Warwick, and A. Ahmed, "Oracy Assessment Toolkit," Faculty of Education, University of Cambridge, http://www.educ.cam.ac.uk/research/projects/oracytoolkit. Accessed April 26, 2018.

It is still a time-consuming process, and so before you decide to assess every child, work out whether you could get a similar level of information that you need from assessing a sample of students instead. In order for your results to be as valid and reliable as possible, spend time with your colleagues looking at a couple of example videos and standardizing your marking against each other's before you mark the rest of the group.

Ultimately, when it comes to assessing oracy, it comes down to what is most useful for you as a teacher, and for your students. It is you, your students, and their parents/caregivers who are the most important audience for oracy assessment information, and there are plenty of formative assessment methods that will support you to make decisions about the oracy teaching, learning, and curriculum within your classroom. Whilst finding a perfect system for summatively assessing oracy is a challenge, you are best placed to assess your students' progress in oracy.

Moreover, if you have been focusing on oracy—deliberately, explicitly, and systematically teaching your students speaking and listening skills—this will be obvious when someone meets one of your students. The proof of the learning that has taken place will be in the children you teach. It will be heard when listening to them speak, seen when watching them in group discussion, felt through the questions they ask and the attentiveness with which they listen. While this may be difficult to bottle up, this is the real reason to teach oracy and we must not lose sight of this.

QUESTIONS TO CONSIDER

- Why do you want to assess oracy, and which assessment method best suits this purpose?
- How do you know your students are making progress in oracy?
- Do your students know their strengths in oracy and what they need to improve?

NOTES

1. P. Black and D. Wiliam, "Inside the Black Box: Raising Standards through Classroom Assessment," *Phi Delta Kappan* 80, no. 2 (October 1998); 139–44, 146–48.

2. N. Mercer, P. Warwick, and Ahmed A. (2017) "An Oracy Assessment Toolkit: Linking Research and Development in the Assessment of Students' Spoken Language Skills at Age 11–12." *Learning and Instruction*, 48, 51–60.

Index

About the Authors

Amy Gaunt and Alice Stott are directors of teaching and learning at Voice 21, a charity committed to raising the status of oracy in education. Voice 21 provides professional and leadership development, school improvement, and curriculum resources to support young people to find their voices for success in education and in life.

Amy and Alice have developed Voice 21's approach to oracy teaching and learning, building on the best practice developed at School 21, a pioneering state school in Stratford, East London. Working with academics and oracy experts at the University of Cambridge, they have developed Voice 21's flagship National Oracy Leaders' program, which aims to equip the next generation of school leaders with expertise and skills to lead oracy in their schools. Alice and Amy have also supported schools across the UK to embed oracy in their practice, and in doing so have put their ideas and approaches to the test in different contexts and settings.

Amy is a primary teacher and previously taught at School 21, where she led the development of oracy practice across the primary school. Having studied languages at university, she has always understood the importance of spoken language in teaching and learning and has spent time teaching internationally as well as teaching English as a foreign language.

Alice is a secondary English teacher by trade and has taught at schools across London. Before joining Voice 21, Alice led oracy in the secondary phase at School 21, developing the explicit and deliberate teaching of oracy across different subjects and ages. Having loved debating as a teenager, and having taught debate at inner-city London schools, Alice is well-aware of the impact oracy can have on young people's confidence and self-esteem.

Made in the USA
San Bernardino, CA
10 November 2019

59701975R00110